Counseling and Psychotherapy

Counseling and Psychotherapy

Korey Maximilian

CLANRYE
INTERNATIONAL
www.clanryeinternational.com

Clanrye International,
750 Third Avenue, 9th Floor,
New York, NY 10017, USA

ISBN: 978-1-63240-900-3

Cataloging-in-Publication Data

Counseling and psychotherapy / Korey Maximilian.
p. cm.
Includes bibliographical references and index.
ISBN 978-1-63240-900-3
1. Counseling. 2. Psychotherapy. 3. Clinical sociology. I. Maximilian, Korey.
BF636.6 .C68 2019
158.3--dc23

For information on all Clanrye International publications
visit our website at www.clanryeinternational.com

CLANRYE INTERNATIONAL

Printed in China.

Contents

Preface

A person may suffer from crises in personal and social life, suffer setbacks and display troublesome behavior, compulsions and emotional turmoil. Counseling is the practice of providing counsel to individuals to empower them to manage personal difficulties and problems. There exists various therapeutic modalities of counseling, such as emotional therapy, existential counseling, grief counseling, grief therapy, marriage counseling, person-centered therapy, rehabilitation counseling, etc. Psychotherapy is the science that is concerned with the employment of psychological methods for the betterment of the mental state and behavior of an individual. Diverse psychotherapy techniques such as one-to-one sessions between a therapist and the afflicted individual, group therapies, therapies involving families, etc. can be employed. The book studies, analyses and uphold the pillars of counseling and psychotherapy and their utmost significance in modern times. Some of the diverse topics covered herein address the varied techniques that fall under these categories. It is an essential guide for therapists, counselors, academicians, students and those who wish to pursue this discipline further.

To facilitate a deeper understanding of the contents of this book a short introduction of every chapter is written below:

Chapter 1- Counseling is the practice of providing counsel or advice to people on matters related to their personal problems and difficulties. The aim of this chapter is to provide an introduction to counseling. It includes vital topics related to counseling and counseling psychology.

Chapter 2- There are different forms of counseling, depending on the issues dealt with, such as career counseling, grief counseling, rehabilitation counseling, marriage counseling, etc. The topics elaborated in this chapter explore these different forms of counseling to provide a comprehensive understanding of the subject matter.

Chapter 3- Counseling empowers individuals, families and groups to achieve good mental health, educational, relationship and career goals. The aim of this chapter is to explore the varied concepts of counseling, such as relationship education, academic advising, self-help, emotional conflict, etc.

Chapter 4- In order to completely understand counseling and counseling methods, it is necessary to study the methodologies of senior peer counseling, online counseling, telephone counseling, suicide prevention, senior peer counseling, etc. This chapter closely examines these methods for a comprehensive understanding.

Chapter 5- Psychotherapy is the practice of using psychological methods for changing a person's behavior and helping him/her overcome problems so as to improve his/her mental health and well-being. This chapter has been carefully written to provide an easy understanding of the different therapies under the scope of psychotherapy, such as art, dance, narrative, music, emotional and family therapy, among others.

Chapter 6- Counseling is aimed at resolving issue of private and professional life and involves planning strategies for stress management, reconciliation, conflict resolution and for improving emotional health. This chapter explores all such aspects of counseling.

Chapter 7- Trauma counseling is a kind of psychotherapy aimed at helping people cope with the emotional, physical, cognitive and spiritual responses to loss. Each person has a unique set of emotional responses to the anticipation of loss, or during and after the trauma. This chapter explores the role of trauma counseling for trauma recovery and discusses about the kinds of trauma and the varied trauma treatment techniques.

Chapter 8- Depression is the state of the mind characterized by an aversion to activity and low spirits that adversely affects the behavior, thoughts, feelings, and the sense of well-being. Counseling can play a significant role in the management of depression. The topics elaborated in this chapter explore the impact of counseling on depression through the inclusion of topics related to the types of depression, effective treatment, techniques of depression, etc.

Chapter 9- Career counseling involved giving advice and guidance regarding career change, career exploration, and career development. Career counselors assists in making good choices of career by putting a person's aptitudes, weaknesses, qualification, hobbies, job prospects, etc. in a broad perspective. This chapter investigates the importance of career counseling in the modern scenario and also discusses about career development and guidance, career counseling process, Holland's Theory, etc.

Finally, I would like to thank the entire team involved in the inception of this book for their valuable time and contribution. This book would not have been possible without their efforts. I would also like to thank my friends and family for their constant support.

Korey Maximilian

1

Introduction to Counseling

Counseling is the practice of providing counsel or advice to people on matters related to their personal problems and difficulties. The aim of this chapter is to provide an introduction to counseling. It includes vital topics related to counseling and counseling psychology.

Counseling is the application of mental health, psychological or human development principles, through cognitive, affective, behavioral or systemic interventions, strategies that address wellness, personal growth, or career development, as well as pathology. Counseling deals with wellness, personal growth, career, and pathological concerns. In other words, counselors work in areas that involve relationships. These areas include intra- and interpersonal concerns related to finding meaning and adjustment in such settings as schools, families, and careers.

Counseling is conducted with persons who are considered to be functioning well and those who are having more serious problems. Counseling meets the needs of a wide spectrum of people. Clients seen by counselors have developmental or situational concerns that require help in regard to adjustment or remediation. Their problems often require short-term intervention, but occasionally treatment may be extended to encompass disorders included in the Diagnostic and Statistical Manual of Mental Disorders of the American Psychiatric Association. Counseling is theory based. Counselors draw from a number of theoretical approaches, including those that are cognitive, affective, behavioral, and systemic. These theories may be applied to individuals, groups, and families. Counseling is a process that maybe developmental or intervening. Counselors focus on their clients' goals. Thus, counseling involves both choice and change. In some cases, "counseling is a rehearsal for action."

Characteristics of Counseling

1. It involves two individual one seeking help and the other a professionally trained person who can help the first. One who seeks help is counselee and the one who provide help is the counselor.
2. There is a mutual respect between the two individuals.
3. It is aimed to bring about desired changes in the individual for self realization and providing assistance to solve problems.
4. The counselor identifies the problems of counselee and helps him to take decision, make a choice or find a direction.
5. It is more than advice giving, solution emerge through thinking that the person does for himself rather than solutions suggested by the counselor.
6. It involves more than offering assistance to find a solution to an immediate problem. Its function is to produce changes in the individual thereby enabling him to deal with the difficulties in a more productive and independent manners.
7. It is a purposeful learning experience for the counselee.
8. Counseling process is structured around the felt needs of the counselee.
9. Main emphasis in the counseling process is on the counselee's self direction and self acceptance.

Principles of Counseling

- Tailor made to the requirement of an individual's problem.
- Emphasizes thinking with the individual.
- Avoid dictatorial attitude.
- Maintains relationship of trust and confidence with the client.
- Client's need is to be put first.
- Everyone participating in the counseling process must feel comfortable.
- Skills of warmth, friendliness, openness and empathy are ingredients of successful counseling process.

- Counselor has to listen attentively, answer question objectively, and reinforce important information.
- Let the client make voluntary informed decision.
- Maintain dignity of individual as individual is primary concern in counseling.

Individual Counseling

Individual counseling is a cooperative and respectful process between therapist and client to facilitate change. As a client, you will be provided a safe, confidential, and supportive environment to pursue the work and change for which you seek.

Engaging in counseling during challenging times takes courage and commitment. The benefits of counseling can lead to greater self-awareness, insight and strength to face the challenges of life, to find hope and meaning.

Relationship Counseling

Relationships are central to our psychological health. Healthy and supportive relationships with friends, family, or partners are associated with increases psychological well being, and reduced levels of depression and stress. However relationships can be complicated, and building and maintaining healthy relationships can be difficult. People seek counseling for couple conflict, relationship breakdown, poor communication, marriage counseling, infidelity, and difficulties in relationships with colleagues, friends, and family members.

Family Counseling

Family therapy can help marriages; couples and families withstand the stress that comes along with some of life's challenges.

Divorce, communication difficulties, parenting, grief and loss are only a few of life stressors that therapy can be useful for.

Trained and experienced therapists can help you improve your communication skills, gain insight into how family of origin issues may relate to your current difficulties and help you improve family relationships.

Feelings of worth can flourish only in an atmosphere where individual differences are appreciated, mistakes are tolerated, communication is open, and rules are flexible – the kind of atmosphere that is found in a nurturing family.

Children and Adolescent Counseling

Counseling can help your child understand, manage and overcome many different personal challenges, such as: anxiety, depression, anger, friendship problems etc.

Importance of Counseling

Counseling can be useful for anyone who wants to explore the way they're thinking or feeling further, as well as for anyone experiencing a problem or issue they are keen to resolve. People may choose to speak to a counselor because they feel they cannot speak to their other half/friends/family about such personal issues, or they may simply wish to speak to a professional with an objective viewpoint.

Common subjects that can be addressed within counseling include the following:

Addictions

Wherever there is a physical addiction to a substance or activity - there is likely to be a psychological addiction too. Counseling aims to relieve the psychological addiction by exploring the root cause while helping to develop new ways of thinking.

Bereavement

Losing a loved one is a difficult event in anyone's life. The loss can bring up a wide range of emotions including guilt and anger. Some people benefit from speaking openly to a counselor about their feelings to help ease the process and resolve any remaining issues they may have.

Bullying

Being the victim of any form of abuse - verbal, emotional or physical - can lead to issues that may affect you all of your life. Counseling can offer victims the chance to seek help from authorities (if appropriate) as well as addressing the psychological repercussions in a safe environment.

Illness

Suffering from a long-term illness such as cancer or dementia can turn anyone's world upside down. Counseling can help sufferers come to terms with their illness while offering emotional support and coping mechanisms.

Mental Health

Suffering from a mental health issue such as schizophrenia or depression can feel incredibly isolating. Counseling looks to discuss the feelings that arise in conjunction with these kinds of mental health issues, as well as overcome any personal challenges or frustrations.

Relationships

Covering all types of relationships, counseling can be used to discuss issues within families, friendships and couples. Problems could involve anything from a poor relationship with a parent, difficulties in a friendship or with a partner, or even your relationships at work.

Trauma

Whether you've been involved in an accident or you have been the victim of abuse, the psychological impact of trauma can last years after the event itself. In a counseling session, trauma victims are encouraged to explore their feelings regarding the incident and look into how these could be resolved or changed.

Other

Feelings of stress, anxiety and low self-esteem are becoming all too common in today's society. Counseling can offer practical advice for overcoming these kinds of issues, as well as allowing you the space to vent your frustrations and feelings.

Types of Therapy

When it comes to counseling there are a range of different approaches, or therapies that can be used. The type of therapy used will depend on your counselor's preferences, the issues you are facing and what type of person you are. Most counselors won't decide on a therapy type until they have found out more about you, the problems you face and the way you think.

The more common types of therapy include:

Art Therapy

Taking an alternative approach to counseling, art therapy encourages clients to use artistic methods to communicate their issues as well as words. This may be in the form of a painting, a sculpture or even a simple drawing. The aim of art therapy is to examine the resulting pieces of art and to interpret their meaning.

Behavioral Therapy

The principle idea behind behavioral therapy is that our behavior is learnt and can essentially be unlearnt. This leads behavioral therapy to focus more on the present as opposed to looking back to the past. This type of therapy is therefore best used with those looking to change their behavior, for example sufferers of addiction or those with a phobia.

Cognitive Therapy

The way we think often leads to changes in our behavior, and cognitive therapy looks to reconcile issues where they begin - in our thoughts. The therapy looks to address any skewed ways of thinking that may be occurring, and eventually aims to replace them with healthier, more positive thought patterns.

Cognitive Behavioral Therapy (CBT)

CBT looks to combine both cognitive therapy and behavioral therapy in order to tackle the thought process and the resulting behavior. Focusing on the present, CBT is a practical therapy that aims to break down problems into smaller, more manageable issues. This therapy is especially useful for those with more specific problems as it addresses each emotion separately.

Eye Movement Desensitization and Reprocessing (EMDR)

EMDR is typically used to treat issues that originated from trauma, though it's starting to be used more widely for issues such as depression and anxiety. The therapy involves recalling the distressing event/feeling while following the therapist's finger as it moves from side to side. The aim is to reduce the intensity of these memories over time.

Humanistic Therapies

The humanistic approach is holistic in style, looking at factors such as free will, creativity and human potential. The therapy type encourages self exploration, with many varieties focusing on the 'here and now'. Therapies that fall under this umbrella include Human Givens therapy, person-centered therapy and Gestalt therapy.

Psychoanalysis

One of the oldest therapies used in psychology; it was Freud who founded the psychoanalytic technique. The therapy takes a different approach to behavioral and cognitive therapies, as it perceives our thoughts to be out of our conscious control. Instead, psychoanalysis believes any psychological issues stem from childhood and need to be addressed in order to be resolved.

Counseling Psychology

Counseling psychology is a broad specialization within professional psychology concerned with using psychological principles to enhance and promote the positive growth, well being, and mental health of individuals, families, groups, and the broader community. Counseling psychologists bring a collaborative, developmental, multicultural, and wellness perspective to their research and practice. They work with many types of individuals, including those experiencing distress and difficulties associated with life events and transitions, decision-making, work/career/education, family and social relationships, and mental health and physical health concerns. In addition to remediation, counseling psychologists engage in prevention, psychoeducation and advocacy. The research and professional domain of counseling psychology overlaps with that of other professions such as clinical psychology, industrial/organizational psychology, and mental health counseling.

Counseling psychology adheres to an integrated set of core values:

- Counseling psychologists view individuals as agents of their own change and regard an individual's pre-existing strengths and resourcefulness and the therapeutic relationship as central mechanisms of change;
- The counseling psychology approach to assessment, diagnosis, and case conceptualization is holistic and client-centered; and it directs attention to social context and culture when considering internal factors, individual differences, and familial/systemic influences; and
- The counseling process is pursued with sensitivity to diverse sociocultural factors unique to each individual.

Counseling psychologists practice in diverse settings and employ a variety of evidence based and theoretical approaches grounded in psychological knowledge. In public agencies, independent practices, schools, universities, health care settings, and corporations, counseling psychologists work in collaboration with individuals to ameliorate distress, facilitate well being, and maximize effective life functioning.

Research and practice are viewed as mutually informative and counseling psychologists conduct research in a wide range of areas, including those of the counseling relationship and other psychotherapeutic processes, the multicultural dimensions of psychology, and the roles of work and mental health in optimal functioning.

Process and Outcome

Counseling psychologists are interested in answering a variety of research questions about counseling process and outcome. Counseling *process* refers to how or why counseling happens and progresses. Counseling *outcome* addresses whether or not counseling is effective, under what conditions it is effective, and what outcomes are considered effective—such as symptom reduction, behavior change, or quality of life improvement. Topics commonly explored in the study of counseling process and outcome include therapist variables, client variables, the counseling or therapeutic relationship, cultural variables, process and outcome measurement, mechanisms of change, and process and outcome research methods. Classic approaches appeared early in the US in the field of humanistic psychology by Carl Rogers who identified the mission of counseling interview as "to permit deeper expression that the client would ordinarily allow himself."

Therapist Variables

Therapist variables include characteristics of a counselor or psychotherapist, as well as therapist technique, behavior, theoretical orientation and training. In terms of therapist behavior, technique and theoretical orientation, research on adherence to therapy models has found that adherence to a particular model of therapy can be helpful, detrimental, or neutral in terms of impact on outcome.

A recent meta-analysis of research on training and experience suggests that experience level is only slightly related to accuracy in clinical judgment. Higher therapist experience has been found to be related to less anxiety, but also less focus. This suggests that there is still work to be done in terms of training clinicians and measuring successful training.

Client Variables

Client characteristics such as help-seeking attitudes and attachment style have been found to be related to client use of counseling, as well as expectations and outcome. Stigma against mental illness can keep people from acknowledging problems and seeking help. Public stigma has been found to be related to self-stigma, attitudes towards counseling, and willingness to seek help.

In terms of attachment style, clients with avoidance styles have been found to perceive greater risks and fewer benefits to counseling, and are less likely to seek professional help, than securely attached clients. Those with anxious attachment styles perceive greater benefits as well as risks to counseling. Educating clients about expectations of counseling can improve client satisfaction, treatment duration and outcomes, and is an efficient and cost-effective intervention.

Counseling Relationship

The relationship between a counselor and client is the feelings and attitudes that a client and therapist have towards one another, and the manner in which those feelings and attitudes are expressed. Some theorists have suggested that the relationship may be thought of in three parts: transference and countertransference, working alliance, and the real—or personal—relationship. Other theorists argue that the concepts of transference and countertransference are outdated and inadequate.

Transference can be described as the client's distorted perceptions of the therapist. This can have a great effect on the therapeutic relationship. For instance, the therapist may have a facial feature that reminds the client of their parent. Because of this association, if the client has significant negative or positive feelings toward their parent, they may project these feelings onto the therapist. This can affect the therapeutic relationship in a few ways. For example, if the client has a very strong bond with their parent, they may see the therapist as a father or mother figure and have a strong connection with the therapist. This can be problematic because as a therapist, it is not ethical to have a more than "professional" relationship with a client. It can also be a good thing, because the client may open up greatly to the therapist. In another way, if the client has a very negative relationship with their parent, the client may feel negative feelings toward the therapist. This can then affect the therapeutic relationship as well. For example, the client may have trouble opening up to the therapist because he or she lacks trust in their parent (projecting these feelings of distrust onto the therapist).

Another theory about the function of the counseling relationship is known as the secure-base hypothesis, which is related to attachment theory. This hypothesis proposes that the counselor acts as a secure base from which clients can explore and then check in with. Secure attachment to one's counselor and secure attachment in general have been found to be related to client exploration. Insecure attachment styles have been found to be related to less session depth than securely attached clients.

Cultural Variables

Counseling psychologists are interested in how culture relates to help-seeking and counseling process and outcome. Standard surveys exploring the nature of counseling across cultures and various ethnic groups include Counseling Across Cultures by Paul B. Pedersen, Juris G. Draguns, Walter J. Lonner and Joseph E. Trimble, Handbook of

Multicultural Counseling by Joseph G. Ponterotto, J. Manueal Casas, Lisa A. Suzuki and Charlene M. Alexander and Handbook of Culture, Therapy, and Healing by Uwe P. Gielen, Jefferson M. Fish and Juris G. Draguns. Janet E. Helms' racial identity model can be useful for understanding how the relationship and counseling process might be affected by the client's and counselor's racial identity. Recent research suggests that clients who are Black are at risk for experiencing racial micro-aggression from counselors who are White.

Efficacy for working with clients who are lesbians, gay men, or bisexual might be related to therapist demographics, gender, sexual identity development, sexual orientation, and professional experience. Clients who have multiple oppressed identities might be especially at-risk for experiencing unhelpful situations with counselors, so counselors might need help with gaining expertise for working with clients who are transgender, lesbian, gay, bisexual, or transgender people of color, and other oppressed populations.

Gender role socialization can also present issues for clients and counselors. Implications for practice include being aware of stereotypes and biases about male and female identity, roles and behavior such as emotional expression. The APA guidelines for multicultural competence outline expectations for taking culture into account in practice and research.

Counseling Ethics

Perceptions on ethical behaviors vary depending upon geographical location, but ethical mandates are similar throughout the global community. Ethical standards are created to help practitioners; clients and the community avoid any possible harm or potential for harm. The standard ethical behaviors are centered on "doing no harm" and preventing harm.

Counselors cannot share any confidential information that is obtained through the counseling process without specific written consent by the client or legal guardian except to prevent clear, imminent danger to the client or others, or when required to do so by a court order. Insurance companies or government programs will also be notified of certain information about your diagnosis and treatment to determine if your care is covered. Those companies and government programs are bound by HIPAA to keep that information strictly confidential.

Counselors are held to a higher standard that most professionals because of the intimacy of their therapeutic delivery. Counselors are not only to avoid fraternizing with their clients. They should avoid dual relationships, and never engage in sexual relationships.

Counselors are to avoid receiving gifts, favors, or trade for therapy. In some communities, it may be avoidable given the economic standing of that community. In cases of children, children and the mentally handicapped, they may feel personally rejected if an offering is something such as a "cookie". As counselors, a judgment call must be made, but in a majority of cases, avoiding gifts, favors, and trade can be maintained.

The National Board for Certified Counselors states that counselors "shall discuss important considerations to avoid exploitation before entering into a non-counseling relationship with a former client. Important considerations to be discussed include amount of time since counseling service termination, duration of counseling, nature and circumstances of client's counseling, the likelihood that the client will want to resume counseling at some time in the future; circumstances of service termination and possible negative effects or outcomes."

Outcome Measurement

Counseling outcome measures might look at a general overview of symptoms, symptoms of specific disorders, or positive outcomes, such as subjective well-being or quality of life. The Outcome Questionnaire-45 is a 45-item self-report measure of psychological distress. An example of disorder-specific measure is the Beck Depression Inventory. The Quality of Life Inventory is a 17-item self-report life satisfaction measure.

Process and Outcome Research Methods

Research about the counseling process and outcome uses a variety of research methodologies to answer questions about if, how, and why counseling works. Quantitative methods include randomly controlled clinical trials, correlation studies over the course of counseling, or laboratory studies about specific counseling process and outcome variables. Qualitative research methods can involve conducting, transcribing and coding interviews; transcribing and/or coding therapy sessions; or fine-grain analysis of single counseling sessions or counseling cases.

Training and Supervision

Professional Training Process

Counseling psychologists are trained in graduate programs. Almost all programs grant a PhD, but a few grant a MCouns, MEd, MA, PsyD or EdD. Most doctoral programs take 5–6 years to complete. Graduate work in counseling psychology includes coursework in general psychology and statistics, counseling practice, and research. Students must complete an original dissertation at the end of their graduate training. Students must also complete a one-year full-time internship at an accredited site before earning their doctorate. In order to be licensed to practice, counseling psychologists must gain clinical experience under supervision, and pass a standardized exam.

In Australia, counseling psychology programs are accredited by the Australia Psychological Society (APS). To become licensed as a counseling psychologist, one must meet the criteria for a psychologist's license: 3 years studying bachelor's degree in Psychology, 4th year Honors degree or Postgraduate Diploma in Psychology, and two-year full-time supervised practice plus 80 hours of professional development. To become a counseling psychologist one must complete a two-year master's degree after obtaining a four-year degree in psychology. There are other avenues available. A substantial component of this master's degree is dedicated to individual psychotherapy, family and couples therapy, group therapy, developmental theory and psychopathology

Training Models and Research

Counseling psychology includes the study and practice of counselor training and counselor supervision. As researchers, counseling psychologists may investigate what makes training and supervision effective. As practitioners, counseling psychologists may supervise and train a variety of clinicians. Counselor training tends to occur in formal classes and training programs. Part of counselor training may involve counseling clients under the supervision of a licensed clinician. Supervision can also occur between licensed clinicians, as a way to improve clinicians' quality of work and competence with various types of counseling clients.

As the field of counseling psychology formed in the mid-20th century, initial training models included Robert Carkuff's human relations training model, Norman Kagan's Interpersonal Process Recall, and Allen Ivey's micro-counseling skills. Modern training models include Gerard Egan's skilled helper model, and Clara E. Hill's three-stage model (exploration, insight, and action). A recent analysis of studies on counselor training found that modeling, instruction, and feedback are common too most training models, and seem to have medium to large effects on trainees.

Supervision Models and Research

Like the models of how clients and therapists interact, there are also models of the interactions between therapists and their supervisors. Edward S. Bordin proposed a model of supervision working alliance similar to his model of therapeutic working alliance. The Integrated Development Model considers the level of a client's motivation/ anxiety, autonomy, and self and other awareness. The Systems Approach to Supervision views the relationship between supervisor and supervised as most important, in addition to characteristics of the supervisor's personal characteristics, counseling clients, training setting, as well as the tasks and functions of supervision. The Critical Events in Supervision model focuses on important moments that occur between the supervisors and supervised.

Problems can arise in supervision and training. First, supervisors are liable for malpractice. Also, questions have arisen as far as a supervisor's need for formal training to be a competent supervisor. Recent research suggests that conflicting, multiple relationships can occur between supervisors and clients, such as that of the client, instructor, and clinical supervisor. The occurrence of racial micro-aggression against Black clients suggests potential problems with racial bias in supervision. In general, conflicts between a counselor and his or her own supervisor can arise when supervisors demonstrate disrespect, lack of support, and blaming.

Vocational Development and Career Counseling

Vocational Theories

There are several types of theories of vocational choice and development. These types include trait and factor theories, social cognitive theories, and developmental theories. Two examples of trait and factor theories, also known as person–environment fit, are Holland's theory and the Theory of Work Adjustment.

John Holland hypothesized six vocational personality/interest types and six work environment types: realistic, investigative, artistic, social, enterprising, and conventional. When a person's vocational interests match his or her work environment types, this is considered congruence. Congruence has been found to predict occupation and college major.

The Theory of Work Adjustment (TWA), as developed by René Dawis and Lloyd Lofquist, hypothesizes that the correspondence between a worker's needs and the reinforced systems predicts job satisfaction, and that the correspondence between a worker's skills and a job's skill requirements predicts job satisfaction. Job satisfaction and personal satisfaction together should determine how long one remains at a job. When there is a discrepancy between a worker's needs or skills and the job's needs or skills, then change needs to occur either in the worker or the job environment.

Social Cognitive Career Theory (SCCT) has been proposed by Robert D. Lent, Steven D. Brown and Gail Hackett. The theory takes Albert Bandura's work on self-efficacy and expands it to interest development, choice making, and performance. Person variables in SCCT include self-efficacy beliefs, outcome expectations and personal goals. The model also includes demographics, ability, values, and environment. Efficacy and outcome expectations are theorized to interrelate and influence interest development, which in turn influences choice of goals, and then actions. Environmental supports and barriers also affect goals and actions. Actions lead to performance and choice stability over time.

Career development theories propose vocational models that include changes throughout the lifespan. Donald Super's model proposes a lifelong five-stage career development process. The stages are growth, exploration, establishment, maintenance, and disengagement. Throughout life, people have many roles that may differ in terms of importance and meaning. Super also theorized that career development is an implementation of self-concept. Gottfredson also proposed a cognitive career decision-making process that develops through the lifespan. The initial stage of career development is hypothesized to be the development of self-image in childhood, as the range of possible roles narrows using criteria such as sex-type, social class, and prestige. During and after adolescence, people take abstract concepts into consideration, such as interests.

Career Counseling

Career counseling may include provision of occupational information, modeling skills, written exercises, and exploration of career goals and plans. Career counseling can also involve the use of personality or career interest assessments, such as the Myers-Briggs Type Indicator, which is based on Carl Jung's theory of psychological type, or the Strong Interest Inventory, which makes use of Holland's theory. Assessments of skills, abilities, and values are also commonly assessed in career counseling.

The problems addressed by counseling psychology are addressed from developmental (lifespan), environmental and cultural perspectives. They include, but are not limited to:

- School and career/work adjustment concerns.
- Making decisions about career and work, and dealing with school-work-retirement transitions.
- Relationship difficulties-including marital and family difficulties.
- Learning and skill deficits.
- Stress management and coping with negative life events.
- Organizational problems.
- Dealing with and adjusting to physical disabilities, disease or injury.
- Personal/social adjustment.
- The development of one's identity.
- Persistent difficulties with relating to other people in general.
- Mental disorders.

References

- Rogers, Carl R. (1947). "Some Observations on the Organization of Personality". American Psychologist. 2: 358. doi:10.1037/h0060883
- What-is-Counselling-A-Search-for-a-Definition: ccpa-accp.ca, Retrieved 10 July 2018
- (OCR), Office for Civil Rights (2014-02-20). "Sharing Information Related to Mental Health". HHS.gov. Retrieved 2017-04-28
- Counselling-definition-characteristics-principles-problems-in-counselling: nsgmed.com, Retrieved 11 June 2018

- Constantine, M. & Sue, D. (2007). Perceptions of racial micro-aggression among black clients in cross-racial studies. Journal of Counseling Psychology, 54(2), 142–153
- Types-counselling: connectionscounselling.com.au, Retrieved 31 March 2018
- Levy, K. N. & Scala, J. (2012). Transference, transference interpretations, and transference-focused psychotherapies. Psychotherapy, 49(3), 391–403. doi:10.1037/a0029371
- What-is-counselling: counselling-directory.org.uk, Retrieved 11 April 2018
- Constantine, M. (2007). Racial micro-aggression against African American clients in cross-racial counseling relationships. Journal of Counseling Psychology, 54(1), 1–16
- Counselling-Psychology: cpa.ca, Retrieved 19 May 2018

2

Different Forms of Counseling

There are different forms of counseling, depending on the issues dealt with, such as career counseling, grief counseling, rehabilitation counseling, marriage counseling, etc. The topics elaborated in this chapter explore these different forms of counseling to provide a comprehensive understanding of the subject matter.

Career Counseling

Career counseling, also known as career guidance, is counseling designed to help with choosing, changing, or leaving a career and is available at any stage in life. One's career is often one of the most important aspects of adulthood, and embarking on a new career, whether for the first time, the second time, or any time thereafter, can be a stressful event, especially when economic difficulties such as recession are a factor. A career counselor can help by outlining and discussing one's potential career options.

Choosing a Career

Choosing a career is an important task, but it may also be a difficult one. It may not be easy to decide what type of job will be the best fit, and since career counseling helps people assess their skills, needs, and desires in order to find a career that works for them, this type of counseling is considered to be an important step to take before deciding on a permanent career. Researching a wide variety of potential careers may be overwhelming, and information on the skill sets and education needed for a particular position may be contradictory or difficult to find. A career counselor will often be able to provide valuable information in these areas and others.

Some of the following questions may be helpful for narrowing one's focus when considering a career change:

- What do I enjoy doing?
- What kinds of activities are fun and fulfilling for me?
- What am I good at?
- What is my skill set?
- What qualifications do I have, such as a degree or experience?
- How much money do I need to make to feel satisfied?
- What jobs are available in the place(s) I'd like to live?
- Do I want to travel?
- What are my values?
- Is it important to me to be of service to others?
- Am I looking for intensely challenging work or something relatively easy?
- Am I willing to do what others tell me without question, or would I rather make most decisions on my own?
- To what degree do I need stability and security?

How Career Counseling Can Help

In a career counseling session, the counselor will help a person explore skills and strengths, consider education levels and give advice about continuing education, and determine interests and personality type. Counselors may also administer an IQ test or an aptitude test. The Myers-Briggs Type Indicator has also been shown to be useful at helping individuals determine possible careers based on personality traits.

Some potential topics of discussion in career counseling:

- Particular skills or talents. In which careers might they be useful?
- The educational commitment required of various careers.
- The potential earnings of various careers.
- The daily working environment. Some people enjoy working in an office, while others might be more successful in a fast-paced or outdoor environment.
- The opportunities for change or advancement in a particular career. Some careers are more flexible than others. Lawyers and doctors, for example, may shift their focus or area of specialty but will generally remain lawyers and doctors.

Other careers or education paths might more allow mobility between positions in a given field.

- The necessary skills/education for a desired career.

Some counselors may also be able to offer advice on how to improve one's position at a job that is, for the most part, enjoyable. For example, possible ways to earn a promotion or the best methods to negotiate a salary adjustment could be discussed.

Key Components of Career Counseling

A Qualified Counselor

A genuine Career Counselor is the essence of right guidance, which is why he/she is the most important element of any career counseling process. Career Counselors are experts in psychology, which means that they should hold at least a post-graduate degree in Psychology/Applied Psychology, and/or a diploma in Counseling Psychology. Career Counselors who give guidance for a particular field, such as engineering, management, hospitality, etc., must be experts in the concerned domain.

A good Career Counselor is a problem solver, a keen listener and observer, and has sufficient knowledge of various fields to guide you in your career decisions.

A Secure Environment

The process of career counseling involves creating a safe and secure environment, where the student feels at ease and is able to discuss his/her life and career, without any hesitation. A part of this secure environment is the assurance of confidentiality of the information shared by the student.

An Agreement Of Trust and Confidence

The Career Counseling process is based on a relationship of trust and confidence between the career counselor and student. In order to help him/her, the counselor may sometimes talk about their emotional and developmental issues, which can be a little stressful. The student and the parent need to place an enormous amount of faith in the Counselor to take care of such matters.

Relevant Psychometric Assessments

Psychometric Testing (Career Assessment) is a scientific and standardized process carried out to evaluate a person's aptitude and personality. Psychometric assessments are a Counselor's tools, which are used to obtain the most important information about a student's behavior, emotional strength, interests, and skills. This information helps to facilitate on what kind of careers would be suitable for him/her.

Benefits

Empirical research attests the effectiveness of career counseling. Professional career counselors can support people with career-related challenges. Through their expertise in career development and labor markets, they can put a person's qualifications, experience, strengths and weakness in a broad perspective while also considering their desired salary, personal hobbies and interests, location, job market and educational possibilities. Through their counseling and teaching abilities, career counselors can additionally support people in gaining a better understanding of what really matters for them personally, how they can plan their careers autonomously, or help them in making tough decisions and getting through times of crisis. Finally, career counselors are often capable of supporting their clients in finding suitable placements/ jobs, in working out conflicts with their employers, or finding the support of other helpful services. It is due to these various benefits of career counseling that policy makers in many countries publicly fund guidance services. For example, the European Union understands career guidance and counseling as an instrument to effectively combat social exclusion and increase citizens' employability.

Co-counseling

Co-counseling is a self-help peer-support system also known as re-evaluation counseling. This form of therapy involves people working in pairs, taking equal time the role of counselor and client. The principle behind this form of therapy is that everyone is born with vast intellectual potential but due to painful memories and suppressed feelings; people tend to behave in certain patterns. By taking turns in giving and receiving attention, practitioners can recover from past distress, argues the Re-evaluation Counseling Community, a group that promotes this type of therapy.

The goal of reciprocal counseling is to achieve empowerment by exploring the roots of personal distress in a supportive environment. The benefits of this method include the acceleration of personal growth and the reduction of stress by talking to a peer, rather than an "expert". Co-counseling is believed to increase skills such as being attentive to the needs of others and is said to be compatible with the 12-step recovery program.

Co-counseling was first used by Harvey Jackins, in the late 1960s. The labor organizer brought home a suicidal co-worker and after carrying for him and supporting him, Jackins came to the conclusion that the only useful thing he could do for him was to listen sympathetically as the man entrusted him with his inner turmoil. Jackins found this intriguing so he began using the method with other acquaintances. Soon the group practicing re-evaluation counseling grew larger and expanded from Seattle down the coast of California. Today, the community that offers courses and training for such therapy sessions has international ramifications.

This type of therapy is recommended for anyone struggling with emotional problems, particularly those recovering from discrimination, prejudice or oppression. The goal of co-counseling is to address the basic human needs like the need to understand and be understood.

Theoretical Framework and Assumptions

The original theory of co-counseling centers on the concept of distress patterns. These are patterns of behavior, that is, behavior that tends to be repeated in a particular type of circumstance, that are irrational, unhelpful or compulsive. The theory is that these patterns are driven by the accumulated consequences in the mind of (not currently) conscious memories of past events in which the person was unable to express or discharge the emotion appropriate to the event. Co-counseling enables release from the patterns by allowing "emotional discharge" of the past hurt experiences. Such cathartic discharge includes crying, warm perspiration, trembling, yawning, laughing and relaxed, non-repetitive talking. In day-to-day life, these "discharging" actions may be limited by social norms, such as, for example, taboos around crying, which are widespread in many cultures.

Having temporary undivided supportive attention from another person often gives rise to strong feelings, apparently towards that person, typically of "falling in love" with them. This is similar to the phenomenon of transference, particularly when one of the partners is felt to have more authority because, for instance, they are more experienced, are teachers of co-counseling, or have authority roles within the organization. The organizations differ in the ways that they handle this. The inability to trust and feel in real relationships is often exacerbated by the pseudo-intimacy of co-counseling, making transference more likely and more dangerous.

Therapeutic Context

Many co-counselors take the view, often quite strongly, that co-counseling is not psychotherapy. In the beginning, this was because Re-evaluation Counseling decided not to draw on any discipline of psychotherapy for its theory and practice, although RC did incorporate some ideas from psychoanalysis such as "unconscious promptings" which Jackins adapted and relabeled "restimulation". A similar view is taken by some non-RC co-counselors who regard psychotherapy as involving specialist techniques used by a therapist on a client and is therefore not peer and the client has little or no control over the process.

Others consider that co-counseling is psychotherapeutic, in that it enables change or therapy to take place in the psyche, soul affect or being of an individual. Co-counseling takes a positive view of the person (i.e. we are all essentially good), considers the mind and body as an integrated whole and acknowledges the value of catharsis; it is regarded as an approach within humanistic psychology, a view that would be rejected by some within RC.

Re-evaluation Counseling

The core organization structure of RC consists of classes and local communities set up by experienced co-counselors, which are in turn organized by regions and country.

The term "re-evaluation" refers to the client's need to rethink their past distress experiences after the emotional hurt in those experiences have been discharged, and thereby regain ("re-emerge" with) their natural intellectual and emotional capacities. The RC organization and literature do not accept the description of its practice as psychotherapy, maintaining instead that the process of developing distress patterns that dissolve through emotional discharge in the context of appreciative attention is simply a natural process that does not imply either psychopathology on the part of the individual or the need for professional treatment. Re-evaluation Counseling regards other forms of "mainstream counseling" and psychotherapy in general as frequently inadequate attempts to bring about relief from distress using methods that do not focus on discharge and re-emergence.

In RC, the client and counselor are expected to work co-operatively, participants are expected to provide non-judgmental active listening and to "contradict" the misinformation or other conditions thought to be associated with distress patterns. RC also engages techniques such as "non-permissive" counseling, in which the counselor intervenes to "interrupt" client patterns without the consent of the client. The structure of RC is one of clearly defined leadership, to encourage clarity in the difficult struggles many people have to achieve breakthroughs against their distresses. RC encourages counselors to think very hard about all possible ways to assist the client in discharging.

RC approaches the issue of feelings between co-counselors by having a strict "no-socializing" rule. RC co-counselors are expected not to socialize or have social or sexual relationships with other co-counselors unless these relationships pre-dated their becoming co-counselors. RC specifically rejects the label "transference" for this phenomenon, as this is seen as part of a "symptomatic" method typical in psychology; the original theory of co-counseling (from RC) teaches that the best thing to do in these circumstances is repeatedly counsel on, and "discharge" about, such feelings. In addition, methods of "getting attention out of distress" are available which help with the difficulty of "switching roles" between counselor and client. When taught correctly, counselors are soon able to grasp the difference between counseling relationships and those from outside life. However, sometimes there is a marked pull to "socialize" or confuse the boundaries of the co-counseling relationship with other types of relationships. This is one reason why many consider a well-organized community of co-counselors with clear rules to be essential in the successful practice of co-counseling.

Re-evaluation Counseling places a high importance on the need to understand and adhere to a comprehensive theory about the nature of the universe and of human beings (known in general as the "Benign Reality"), the best ways of assisting the discharge process and of pro-liberation attitudes in co-counseling. RCers believe that, when taken together, these enable the counselor to keep a clear picture of the client's "re-emergence" and are therefore very effective. People disagreeing with the theoretical perspective are asked to think and discharge on the points at issue before actively challenging such perspectives. The main aim is to provide a safe, stable and supportive atmosphere within which people can client skillfully and also lead "re-emergent lives" where they are not dependent in a therapeutic sense, but instead become more energetic and effective (a state known as "zestfulness" in RC).

Co-Counseling International

Co-Counseling International (CCI) was started in 1974 as a breakaway from Re-evaluation Counseling by John Heron, who was at the time director of the Human Potential Research Project, University of Surrey UK, and Tom Sargent and Dency Sargent from Hartford, Connecticut, United States. Unlike other breakaways from RC, which involved changes of leadership but otherwise continued to practice in similar ways to

RC, the CCI break was ideological, and CCI developed in significantly different ways. The differences are in practice, theory and organization.

In practice, the client in CCI co-counseling is wholly in charge of the session. In other words, client and counselor do not work co-operatively. The counselor only intervenes in accordance with one of three levels of "contract"—free attention, normal and intensive—which are defined in CCI's principles. The only requirement of the counselor is that they give "free attention" (that is, full supportive attention) to the client. The other two contracts constitute invitations to the counselor to make interventions from within those permitted if they feel it is appropriate. The intensive contract can be similar to the RC way of working, although the counselor is still not permitted to intervene as flexibly as in RC.

The original theory of co-counseling is taught in the CCI fundamentals training courses, and participants learn techniques for releasing, or "discharging", emotions. However, the theory is not seen as a constraint within CCI, and co-counselors draw on the whole range of psychotherapeutic theory and methods including analytical, cognitive-behavioural and transpersonal as well as humanistic approaches. The principal constraint is that the client must be able to work self-directly.

Organizationally, CCI is a peer network with no core structure. Local and national networks have a variety of organization. Classes and activities are organized by individuals or groups acting self-directly. John Heron's status within the network has always been as an equal member, although inevitably as a founder member and activist for some 15 years and the person who developed much of the thinking behind CCI, there was a certain amount of transference on him. Heron now lives in New Zealand and is involved with the CCI network there.

CCI approaches the issue of personal relationships between co-counselors as a matter for raising awareness. CCI co-counselors may and do have the whole range of personal relationships with other co-counselors. However, new co-counselors are encouraged not to develop new non-co-counseling relationships with other co-counselors until they have more experience and experienced co-counselors will often have people with whom they only have a co-counseling relationship. Teachers of co-counseling are strongly discouraged from having sexual relationships with people they have taught.

Relations Between CCI and RC

The existence of other co-counseling organizations is generally not mentioned in RC, and RC co-counselors are often not aware of their existence.

Amongst those within RC who know about it, CCI is often seen as an "attack organization" and was specifically condemned as such in many private and public conversations by Jackins, who claimed that Heron had started it against a specific agreement not to, and in breach of RC guidelines he had previously agreed to. In turn, Heron and many of his supporters claimed that RC was authoritarian and cult-like, and later, that Jackins engaged in sexual abuse of clients. RC supporters parried that CCI fostered a sexually-liberal atmosphere that blurred the boundaries of co-counseling and relationships.

The history of co-counseling including its origins with RC is normally taught on CCI Fundamentals courses. CCI, by its nature, has no corporate opinion about RC, and individual CCI co-counselors have their own views. Most CCI co-counselors have a benevolent view toward RC, regarding it as a different, alternative approach to co-counseling. Membership of RC is not a bar to membership of CCI, and a few people manage to do both despite the RC ban.

Co-counseling Initiatives

- Focusing Partnerships. Co-counseling based on the focusing technique of Eugene Gendlin.
- The Association of Karen Horney Psychoanalytic Counselors were the original publishers of *The Barefoot Psychoanalyst*, which allies the practice of co-counseling with the theories of Karen Horney. In 1987, the association became The Institute for Self-Analysis, a member of the International Karen Horney Society.
- Dror Co-Counseling was founded in Israel in 1998.
- Peer Listeners was an organization set up following the resignation of Belgian Daniel Le Bon from RC in 1989.

Disciplinary Counseling

A disciplinary counseling session is a meeting between a supervisor and employee. It may focus on a specific work place incident, or may be the result of a performance appraisal. A particular aspect of the employee's performance or conduct may have been identified by the supervisor as requiring attention, or the employee's overall performance or conduct may require adjustment. The counseling process may be initiated and executed by the supervisor and is not considered disciplinary. It is an opportunity for face-to-face communication between the supervisor and the employee, conducted in private, and is intended to have a constructive goal of providing feedback to the employee to correct the problem.

Counseling is an important supervisory skill required as often as any other interaction facing the supervisor. In most cases counseling is a necessary step preceding disciplinary action.

Existential Counseling

Existential counseling helps people come to terms with human issues we all face at some time, such as loneliness and isolation, anxiety, death and loss, freedom, choice and responsibility, meanings and values. These are some of the themes which, when we reflect on them, may help us to understand the context of the problems and challenges we face as human beings.

Questions that Existential Counseling Explore

- What does it mean to be alive?
- What is my relationship to myself and to other people?
- What are my responsibilities to myself and other people?
- What do I value?

- What is my true potential?
- What would it be like to choose my own way of living?

Benefits of Existential Therapy

Existential therapy explores the unfolding nature of human experience, and brings a curiosity to what it means to be human. It also emphasizes the relational aspect of being human i.e. that everything we do is dependent on the context of our lives and the environment we inhabit. It challenges us to make the most of our lives, by facing the choices that lie before us. Then, with increased clarity and insight, we are better equipped to face and solve the issues we experience in life.

Grief Counseling

Grief counseling refers to a specific form of therapy, or a focus in general counseling with the goal of helping the individual grieve and address personal loss in a healthy manner. Grief counseling is offered individually by psychologists, clergy, counselors or social workers, in groups led by professionals, as well as informal support groups offered by churches, community groups, or organizations devoted to helping individuals grieve specific losses.

Specific tasks of grief counseling include emotional expression about the loss (which can include a wide range of feelings), accepting the loss, adjusting to life after the loss, and coping with the changes within oneself and the world after the loss. Typical feelings experienced by individuals, and addressed in grief counseling, include sadness, anxiety, anger, loneliness, guilt, relief, isolation, confusion, or numbness. Behavioral changes may also be noticed, such as being disorganized, feeling tired, having trouble concentrating, sleep problems, appetite changes, vivid dreams, or daydreaming about the deceased.

The purpose of grief counseling is to help individuals work through the feelings, thoughts, and memories associated with the loss of a loved one. Although grieving can occur for other types of loss as well (such as loss of goals, ideals, and relationships), grief counseling is generally directed toward positive adjustment following loss after the death of a loved one.

Grief counseling helps the individual recognize normal aspects of the grieving or mourning process, cope with the pain associated with the loss, feel supported through the anxiety surrounding life changes that may follow the loss, and develop strategies for seeking support and self-care.

Grieving is a normal life process—an adjustment reaction to a loss. Grief counseling is meant to facilitate that normal process. No specific precautions are warranted. However, there are certain circumstances in which complications to the normal grieving process may occur. These circumstances may involve the loss of a child, or the loss of a loved one due to an accident or homicide, for example.

In these cases of complicated grieving, more extreme responses to the loss may be observed, depending on the individual's capacity for coping, personal resiliency, and support system. For example, if the individual feels isolated, he may be at greater risk for severe depressive symptoms or a suicide attempt. Alternatively, if the survivors feel rage or anger over the loss, there may be a risk of harm to others.

Grief counseling helps the individual work through the feelings associated with the loss of another, accept that loss, determine how life can go on without that person, and consolidate memories in order to be able to move forward. Grief counseling also provides information about the normal grieving process, to help individuals understand that many of the symptoms and changes they are experiencing are a normal, temporary reaction to loss. For some individuals, the primary focus of grief counseling is to help identify ways to express feelings about the loss that the person has been unable to express on his or her own. Individuals who seek grief counseling may be experiencing an emotional numbness, or a residual shock in reaction to the loss, and need assistance to return to a normal life. In those cases, grief counseling will focus on helping the individual get in touch with those feelings and become more active in the daily routine. This often requires accepting the loss as a reality.

For some people, grieving may initially be so extreme that physical and psychological symptoms may be experienced, while other people appear to experience no symptoms whatsoever, similar to the numbness described above. Activities of daily living may feel overwhelming to an individual who has experienced a loss. In these cases, grief counseling may focus on specific coping skills to help the individual resume some normalcy in his or her daily routine. For example, if sleep patterns are disrupted, grief counseling may include consultation with the individual's physician to assist with temporary strategies to increase sleep. If the individual is having trouble getting to work on time, behavioral strategies may be used as an interim measure to help the person return to aspects of normal daily life.

Additional work in grief counseling may involve identifying ways to let go or say good-bye if the individual has not been able to do so successfully. Therapeutic letters may be a helpful mechanism to express thoughts that were not conveyed prior to the death. Dreams are frequently experienced by survivors, and these can be a focus in grief counseling as well. The dreams can often be a way of consolidating the memories about the deceased.

Goals of Grief Counseling

Acceptance of the Reality of Loss

Grief doesn't always hit you like a ton of bricks. Sometimes, you feel nothing or a sense of numbness after a major loss. You may go on as if nothing has happened, not fully realizing or accepting what has happened. Even if you feel overwhelmed by emotion, you may feel disconnected from the reason you feel that way. So, the first task of grief, and thus the first goal of grief counseling, is to help you understand with all your being that you've suffered a major loss.

Identifying and Dealing with Trauma

Before you can get to the grief process, your counselor needs to help you identify the parts of your experience that were traumatic. These may include: witnessing the death, seeing the dead body, or other sense experiences surrounding your loved one's death. Once you know what those experiences are, you can describe them, discuss them, and your grief counselor can help you get past them and on to the task of grieving.

Talking Freely about your Loved one

If you don't have anyone to share your grief with, a grief counselor can provide an outlet for your grief. On the other hand, if you're grieving in a fishbowl with friends and family judging your every move, you may need someone like your counselor with whom you can share your personal feelings without worry of saying the wrong thing. Talking freely about your feelings and sharing thoughts and feelings about your relationship with your loved one can be a tremendous relief.

Experiencing and Expressing Emotions

Perhaps you haven't yet felt the sting of the loss you've just experienced. Some people can go months or even years before they experience their feelings about the loss. In the meantime, they continue feeling numb and distant from others. Others feel a jumble of emotions so intensely they can't make sense of them. One of the goals of grief counseling is to express those emotions in whatever way works best for you.

Overcoming Guilt

Guilt, in most cases, is not a healthy emotion to hang onto. Yet, many people feel guilty for things they've said or done or for things they've failed to say or do before their loved one passed. It's important to identify those guilt feelings. Your grief counselor can help you see the futility of burying yourself in should-haves and shouldn't-haves. They can help you find more constructive ways to deal with the reality that no relationship is absolutely perfect.

Coping with Life Changes

When you lose someone who's been close to you, your life necessarily changes. At the least, you won't be able to share happy times with them again. At the most, your entire daily life will be in a state of upheaval because you shared almost every waking moment.

Without them, your life will change, and with that change comes additional losses, such as the loss of a morning routine. Grief counseling can help you examine those changes and find new ways to live your life.

Building a Support System

If the person you lost was your primary support system, you'll likely need to build up your support for daily living. What often happens when a spouse dies is that you now have to do the tasks that you once relied on your spouse to do. You may now have to file insurance papers, manage a budget, or do the cooking and housekeeping chores that you've never done before. This goes much more smoothly after your counselor helps you find community resources and encourages you to build stronger community ties.

Grief Counseling Techniques

Grief counselors use a variety of techniques to help you experience, understand, and move through the grief process. The following grief counseling techniques are just a few of the ones your therapist might use.

Talking Privately in a Quiet Place

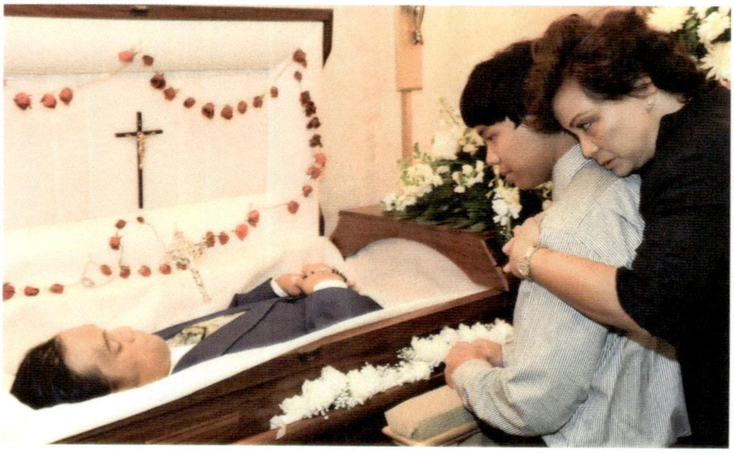

Trying to deal with death in a rushed, noisy atmosphere is extremely unproductive. It's too hard to get down to the serious emotions and challenges that are a part of grief. Of course, most counseling does happen in a quiet, private place. Yet, you may feel hurried to get to your appointment and rushed once you get there. If so, you can set up online grief counseling then so you can talk in private wherever you feel most comfortable.

Describing the Moment of Loss

The moment of loss may have been quiet or traumatic. Describing that moment completely, using sense words like "I heard" or "I saw" allows you to re-experience the loss. As you do, your counselor can put it into perspective while giving you support for feeling the emotions that come up for you as you remember. This also helps them identify trauma, which can then be dealt with before the grief.

Discussing Funeral Arrangements

You might think, "Why would I talk about the funeral arrangements with my grief counselor? What do they have to do with that?" The truth is that the funeral or memorial service that you and/or others set up to honor your loved one is an important event in the grieving process. As you talk about it, you can express your feelings about this last farewell and what you want it to be like. You may even be able to identify ways you want to change the service to give the deceased your full respect.

Using the Right Words

If you pay attention to what your counselor says to you, you might notice that one of their grief counseling techniques is to use the words it's important for you to hear. For example, they'll be sure to use the past tense when talking about your loved one. They'll say their name frequently. They'll also use words that may be very hard for you to hear at first, such as forms of the word "to die."

Checking for Signs of Depression

Each time you see your grief counselor, they'll probably ask you at least a few questions to make sure you aren't falling into a deep depression. They may ask how you're sleeping and how much you're eating. They may ask whether you feel unexplained physical pain. They might cover different depression symptoms at different appointments with you to ensure they aren't missing anything.

Talking About Past Losses

One technique counselors often use is to prompt you to talk about similar situations from the past and how you dealt with them. In the case of grief, your counselor might ask you to remember how you coped when you faced death earlier in your life. Then, they can support you in repeating the things that helped before, and teach you new ways of coping to replace old methods that made things worse.

Boosting Self Esteem

Your self-esteem is the way you feel about yourself, but it may be tied up with what you perceived that your loved one thought of you. If you always relied on them to say or do things that made you feel beautiful, intelligent, or capable, you might need an extra boost of self-esteem after they pass on. Your grief counselor can teach you ways to improve your self-confidence and learn to find validation within yourself.

Giving Permission To Grieve

Many people find it hard to give themselves permission to grieve. They may see it as a sign of weakness, selfishness, or incompetence. Yet, grieving is a crucial part of saying goodbye to a loved one who has died. Your counselor can help you find it within you to give yourself the permission you need to feel and express your feelings and not be so perfect all the time.

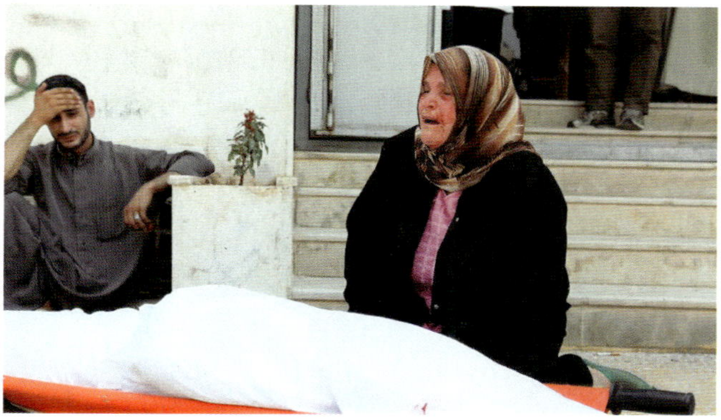

Setting Realistic Goals

Goal-setting is a part of almost every kind of therapy. Because grief involves so many life changes for most people, setting goals for your new life is especially important. You may find yourself setting unrealistic goals, though, as you try to push through your grief faster. However, you need to be cautious, so you don't overwhelm yourself. Setting unreachable goals makes you feel like a failure when you can't accomplish them. It can also be a way of avoiding the natural grief process. Talk out your plans with your counselor so they can help you determine the right goals to work towards right now.

Writing A Letter

Your therapist might suggest you write a letter to the deceased to tell them how you feel about losing them. They might also suggest that you tell them about how your life is now and the goals you're working toward for the future. This exercise can help you get back in touch with the feelings of love you have for them. It can help you resolve issues that linger in your mind, too.

Journaling

Journaling is like letter-writing, but the intended audience is you. You remind yourself of good times, reason out problems, write poems to express your feelings, draw pictures that remind you of your loved one, or include mementos of happy times you shared. It's a place to say whatever you want, just as you can with your therapist. It's also a habit that can serve you well after your grief counseling ends.

Reading Assignments

Reading about grief helps you understand the process. It also reminds you that what you're going through is not only common but perfectly acceptable as well. In short, it normalizes grief. Your grief counselor might suggest specific books for you to read between sessions.

Creating a Memory Book

Creating a memory book is a craft project you can do to help you remember your loved one in a helpful way. You can make it alone or ask family members and friends to contribute to it. This is one of the grief techniques that are not only emotionally healthy, but it can be enjoyable as well.

Art Therapy

Expressive art therapy, of course, is a wonderful way to show how you feel about your loved one who has passed. A counselor who has certification in art therapy can guide you in creating artistic works that are full of emotion and meaning. Then, when you finish with the art, you can hang it in a special place, give it away, sell it, or simply set it aside for your remembrance ritual.

Imagining a Resolution of Unfinished Business

Grief is hard for anyone, but it can be especially difficult to move on from a relationship that was in crisis when your loved one died. Perhaps you have an issue that you can't forget because it feels unfinished. There's no way for that problem to be resolved in real life now. However, you can imagine what would happen if you were able to resolve it. This grief counseling technique helps you put your relationship into perspective. If you imagine a positive resolution, it can give you amazing peace.

Empty Chair Technique

The empty chair technique is one that is used in several types of therapy. All you do is face an empty chair, imagine another person is sitting in it, and tell them what you want to say to them. In the case of grief counseling, you would imagine the deceased were alive and sitting in that chair. You can say anything you want to them. You can show them feelings that range from bitterness to love. The empty chair technique is another way to find resolution to unfinished business, but it can also be quite cathartic.

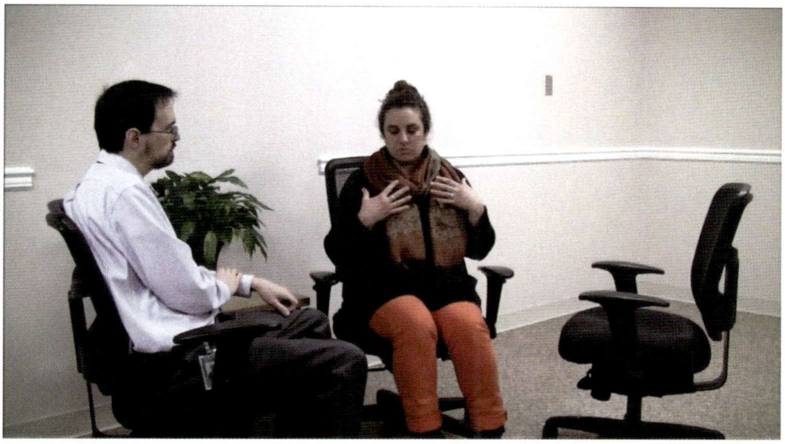

Role Playing New Situations

Role playing is a technique you might have used in family counseling or couples therapy. Your grief counselor might also use it to help you find your way through new life situations. You can be yourself while the counselor plays the part of an employer, a friend, or a community leader, for example. Or, you can reverse roles. Then, you can play out what it would be like to be in a situation you've never had to deal with before.

Creating Remembrance Rituals

Sometimes, the only way to move on is to give yourself a specific time and activity to help you remember your loved one. As a part of your grief therapy, you can come up with a ritual that you do once every month at first and eventually do only once a year. This might involve looking at photos and/or videos of your loved one, for example. You put these reminders away for most of the time, but you take them out at a specific time to pay honor to the deceased.

Marriage Counseling

Marriage counseling, also called couples therapy, is a type of psychotherapy. Marriage counseling helps couples of all types recognize and resolve conflicts and improve their relationships. Through marriage counseling, you can make thoughtful decisions about rebuilding and strengthening your relationship or going your separate ways.

Marriage counseling is often provided by licensed therapists known as marriage and family therapists. These therapists have graduate or postgraduate degrees — and many choose to become credentialed by the American Association for Marriage and Family Therapy (AAMFT).

Marriage counseling is often short term. Marriage counseling typically includes both partners, but sometimes one partner chooses to work with a therapist alone. The specific treatment plan depends on the situation.

Marriage counseling can help couples in all types of intimate relationships — regardless of sexual orientation or marriage status.

Some couples seek marriage counseling to strengthen their partnership and gain a better understanding of each other. Marriage counseling can also help couples who plan to get married. Premarital counseling can help couples achieve a deeper understanding of each other and iron out differences before marriage.

In other cases, couples seek marriage counseling to improve a troubled relationship. You can use marriage counseling to help with many specific issues, including:

- Communication problems
- Sexual difficulties

- Conflicts about child rearing or blended families
- Substance abuse
- Anger
- Infidelity

Marriage counseling might also be helpful in cases of domestic abuse. If violence has escalated to the point that you're afraid, however, counseling alone isn't adequate. Contact the police or a local shelter or crisis center for emergency support.

There are many different approaches to marriage counseling, which may be used alone or combined with other methods by the therapist. Among the oldest is the psychodynamic approach, which attributes problems within a marriage to the unresolved conflicts and needs of each spouse. Each client's personal history and underlying motivations are central to this mode of therapy. Therapists using this approach apply the principles of psychoanalysis in their treatment; they may either treat both marriage partners individually, or treat one spouse in collaboration with another therapist who treats the other.

Marriage counseling that follows a systems approach stresses the interaction between partners as the origin of marital difficulties, rather than their actions or personality. Behavior and communication patterns are analyzed as well as the interlocking roles portrayed by the couple or members of the family. Family members may be conditioned to consistently play "the strong one" or "the weak one," or such other roles as "scapegoat," "caretaker," or "clown." Although initially it may seem that only one member of a family system is troubled, on closer inspection his or her difficulties are often found to be symptomatic of an unhealthy pattern in which all the members play an active part. Systems theory is actually an umbrella term for a range of therapies, and systems-oriented counseling may take a variety of forms, including both short-and long-term therapy.

A popular individual treatment approach also used in marriage counseling is Rogerian or client-centered therapy, also referred to as humanistic therapy. Here, the emphasis is on communication and the open sharing of feelings. Through specially formulated exercises, couples work on improving their speaking and listening skills and enhancing their capacity for emotional honesty. Another widely employed mode of marriage counseling is based on a behavioral approach, in which marital problems are treated as dysfunctional behaviors that can be observed and modified. Couples are made aware of destructive behavior patterns, often by systematically recording their behavior until certain patterns emerge. The therapist then coaches them in various modifying strategies with the goal of achieving positive, mutually reinforcing interactions. Behavior-oriented therapy also focuses on improving a couple's problem-solving and conflict-resolution skills.

Marriage counselors may conduct therapy sessions with both spouses, treating one as the primary client and the other one only occasionally, while another therapist treats the other spouse. An increasing number of therapists counsel couples in pairs, with married therapists sometimes working together as a team. Theoretically, the relationship between the co-therapists is supposed to serve as a model for their clients. Marriage counseling in groups, which is becoming increasingly common, offers clients some of the same advantages that group therapy offers individuals. Sex counseling, which had previously been part of marital therapy, emerged as an independent field following the pioneering work of William Masters and Virginia Johnson in the 1950s and 1960s. Couples seeking treatment for sexual dysfunction have the option of working with a sex therapist.

Marriage counseling is usually practiced by licensed individuals with specialized training in psychology, psychiatry, and counseling, or by persons without such training, including members of the clergy. The first marriage counseling centers were established in the 1930s, and the American Association of Marriage and Family Therapy (formally the American Association of Marriage Counselors) was founded in 1942.

Benefits of Marriage Counseling

You get unstuck

Marriage counseling invites you to step outside of your life for one hour and focus on your relationship. Your therapist acts a mediator, providing you and your partner with the guidance you need to listen to each other uninterruptedly.

Counseling creates an environment encouraging open, two-way communication. When we're stuck in old patterns we often forget that whatever we're doing isn't working.

We create stagnant energy in our relationships when we're unaware of these patterns, and we end up feeling disconnected. Marriage counseling helps you overcome the lack of intimate communication so you can better understand each other and create meaningful change.

You Realize your Fears

You get past the surface level issues and repetitive arguments. These repetitive arguments are symptoms of underlying issues often related to fear.

Surface level issues typically fall into certain topics in your life, such as finances, sex and parenting. When you get past the symptomatic issues, you can finally deal with the underlying unmet needs and emotional injuries.

Your underlying fears and perceptions manifest in very particular (and often recurring) ways, and a therapist can help you see how this happens for you in your marriage. If you can get to what lies beneath the negative patterns in your relationship, your arguments will eventually dissipate.

You Commit to Growth

When you go to marriage counseling, you're investing in something that will grow. Just as neglecting your health and finances could lead to illness and debt, neglecting your relationship could lead to divorce or an unhappy marriage at best.

When you invest in counseling, what you're really investing in is the will to change. Accepting help from someone else in an intimate area of your life is a wonderful thing. Your willingness to change and ask for help and guidance is a big step in a better direction.

You Deepen Intimacy and Connection

Marriage counseling helps you deepen intimacy and connection. Your ability to have meaningful conversations with your partner is typically interrupted by work, kids, and even feeling tired after a long day. Marriage counseling creates space for deeper emotional intimacy in your relationship. This new awareness infiltrates your sex life, connectedness, and your overall happiness.

You get a Personal Trainer, but for your Relationship

You have a health professional to point out your blind spots. Your therapist is focused directly on your relationship. They are able to identify fears and patterns you're not aware of so that you can realize *your part* in the recurring issues.

You're Held Accountable

You're required to put change into practice. Therapists will often give you homework and experiments to take into your life. Putting what you've learned into practice is key to parting ways with old perceptions and patterns to create lasting change.

You Learn to Forgive and Let go

Marriage counseling always leads you somewhere different and somewhere better. You get the benefit of forgiveness and release. You come out of therapy as someone who has learned a new language. You've learned how to communicate and connect in a new way.

Rehabilitation Counseling

Rehabilitation counseling is a process that is designed to assist people with disabilities in accomplishing their goals and in achieving independence and full participation in all aspects of community life. Rehabilitation counseling is also a recognized counseling profession, with a long history and established professional credentialing procedures. It is variously conceptualized as a specialty within counseling, as a specialty within rehabilitation, and as a separate profession.

The historical roots of rehabilitation counseling date back to the early 1900s. During World War I, many military personnel returned home with disabilities, and rehabilitation programs were established to assist them in returning to productive civilian roles. The Soldier Rehabilitation Act was enacted in 1918. Simultaneously, efforts were under way in several different states to assist workers who had been injured in industrial accidents in returning to work, the roots of contemporary worker's compensation programs. Finally, the Smith-Fess Act of 1920 established a vocational rehabilitation program for civilians with disabilities. All of these initiatives evolved into the extensive network of government, private-nonprofit, and private-for-profit agencies and programs to assist people with disabilities. Rehabilitation counseling plays a central role within these agencies and programs, providing assessment, counseling, and coordination of rehabilitation services.

To illustrate the rehabilitation process, a spinal cord injury may occur through a variety of events, such as a motor vehicle crash, a fall, a diving accident, or a gunshot wound, resulting in paralysis below the level of the injury. An individual who sustains a spinal cord injury will often be taken to a trauma center and will initially be treated through medical interventions to manage the acute condition and any complications that may result, and also to limit long-term adverse consequences. After the medical condition is stabilized, the individual will often be transferred to a rehabilitation unit within the hospital, where a variety of disciplines will assist the individual in recovering function and dealing with the limitations that will remain in the long term. The individual will learn new ways to perform tasks, for example, moving from place to place using a wheelchair, driving a car through the use of hand controls, and performing basic living tasks, such as eating and grooming. Many aspects of the life of the individual, as well as the lives of family and friends, will be affected. For example, the individual may no longer be able to work in the same occupation that had been a primary source of family income and personal identity. In some instances, it may be possible to help an employer identify accommodations that will make it possible for the individual to again perform the job. In other instances, the individual may need assistance in making new plans for the future. Every aspect of life may be affected, and rehabilitation professionals can participate in assisting the individual in recovering function, identifying and implementing accommodations, planning for the future, and maximizing independence and quality of life.

Rehabilitation services are provided in a variety of agencies and programs, and rehabilitation counseling is a part of the programming in many of these settings. Government programs providing rehabilitation services include agencies at the federal level (e.g., the Department of Veterans Affairs, where rehabilitation counseling is practiced in both the Veterans Benefits Administration, which coordinates disability and rehabilitation benefits, and in the Veterans Health Administration, which includes the Veterans Industries/ Compensated Work Therapy Program that provides rehabilitation services to veterans with disabilities); the state level (the State-Federal Vocational Rehabilitation agencies, which exist in all states and jurisdictions in the United States, along with separate agencies for people with blindness and low vision in a number of states); and the county and city levels (e.g., local government agencies providing rehabilitation and long-term support services for people with developmental disabilities and with severe and persistent mental illness).

Rehabilitation Counseling Practice

Guiding Principles

Many of the guiding principles, philosophies, and values underlying the practice of rehabilitation counseling are shared by counseling in general, as well as by other helping professions. The belief in the worth and dignity of all people, including people with disabilities, is particularly important. Following from the belief in the worth of all people, rehabilitation counseling practice is dedicated to facilitating full access to opportunities for participation in all aspects of community life and to the pursuit of individually determined goals, consistent with the opportunities available to others in society. Following from the belief in the dignity of all people, rehabilitation counseling attempts to empower people with disabilities in achieving control over their own lives and the opportunities and goals that they choose to pursue. Consistent with this value is an emphasis on informed choice in rehabilitation counseling practice, viewing people with disabilities as equal collaborators in the rehabilitation counseling process and assisting them in obtaining and processing the information that they need to make their own decisions regarding services, interventions, and goals.

Also similar to counseling in general, rehabilitation counseling has a long tradition of going beyond limitations and problems to focus on the strengths of individuals with disabilities and helping them to build on those strengths in overcoming the difficulties that they face in accomplishing their goals and living high-quality lives. In addition, the ecological perspective in rehabilitation counseling advocates a focus not only on the individual but also on environmental contexts, in assessing difficulties brought to rehabilitation counseling and in the planning of goals, services, and interventions.

Another value held in contemporary rehabilitation counseling practice, as specified in the CRCC definition of rehabilitation counseling, is the importance of pursuing "personal, career, and independent living goals in the most integrated settings possible." Historically, career and independent living goals for people with disabilities, particularly for those with significant cognitive disabilities and severe and persistent mental illness, were often focused on segregated settings. Large numbers of people with disabilities were congregated in large work environments, such as sheltered workshops, and in large living environments, such as skilled nursing facilities, community-based residential facilities, halfway houses, and group homes. Contemporary practice emphasizes the pursuit of employment goals in regular work environments in business and industry, where individuals with disabilities will be integrated with the regular workforce, with necessary supports provided to facilitate success. Similarly, integrated living environments would be exemplified by one or two people with disabilities living in a regular community apartment building or complex, together with nondisabled people, with necessary supports provided.

Rehabilitation Counseling Process

The rehabilitation counseling process is generally consistent with the counseling process in general. The process is collaborative, with rehabilitation counselors and individuals with disabilities jointly assessing and identifying needs; establishing personal, career, and independent living goals; identifying barriers to accomplishing those goals; identifying needed services and interventions to overcome the barriers and accomplish the goals; organizing those services and interventions into a service plan; and implementing and evaluating the progress and success of the plan. Individuals with disabilities often seek rehabilitation counseling at times of change or crisis, such as the onset of a disability, changes in condition or functioning associated with disability, or times of transition (e.g., discharge from a hospital, completion of high school and moving on to adult and community life, struggles with the demands of an education or training program, the illness or death of a caretaker, or termination from a job). At times of crisis, assistance will often be required through rehabilitation counseling in processing those changes and their implications, identifying and accessing community resources, and finding new ways to meet needs, which may precede the establishment and pursuit of personal, career, and independent living goals.

As in counseling in general, in rehabilitation counseling the emphasis is on the counseling relationship and developing a strong working alliance between rehabilitation counselors and individuals with disabilities. As is also true in counseling in general, eclectic approaches to counseling are common, with counselors drawing from a number of different counseling theories and techniques in their practice. Because of the emphasis on facilitating career, independent living, and life decisions, trait-and-factor theories and concepts are often applied. Given their emphasis on helping people build on strengths, cognitive-behavioral theories and practices can be beneficial in guiding people to develop skills for coping with difficulties and become masters of their own destinies to greater degrees.

Given the complexity of needs that is often associated with disabilities, the involvement of many different professionals, programs, and services is often required and, as a result, service coordination and case management are often critical components of the rehabilitation counseling process. In addition, given the common focus on career goals, important components of the process are often job development and placement and the facilitation of independent job-seeking efforts on the part of individuals served.

Some functions and tasks are unique or are emphasized to a greater degree in rehabilitation counseling practice than in counseling in general. Given the prominence of ecological perspectives, and the belief that problems related to disability reside in large part in the physical and social environments in which people with disabilities live and work, advocacy is emphasized. This includes both advocating for people with disabilities and assisting them in their efforts at self-advocacy. Related to advocacy, rehabilitation counselors may be called upon to consult with business, industry, and other organizations in facilitating accessibility and accommodating the needs of people with disabilities, including the identification of assistive technology that may be used. In addition, rehabilitation counselors may be called upon to assist in legal proceedings, such as workers' compensation, personal injury, and divorce cases, to assess the impact of disability on earning potential so that appropriate compensation can be determined. Similarly, in life care planning, rehabilitation counselors may be called upon to assess the life-long service needs of individuals with disabilities, along with the costs of obtaining those services, in order to determine appropriate insurance settlements following the onset of a disability.

Pregnancy Options Counseling

The form of counseling meant for providing knowledge and support regarding pregnancy is known as pregnancy options counseling. The women who usually seek such kind of counseling are the ones, which are having a case of unintended pregnancy. A major factor contributing to the rise in the number of unintended pregnancies is limited access to family planning resources. Furthermore, the misuse of birth control is another main factor responsible for it.

Pregnancy options counselor plays a significant role in helping woman deal with such kind of pregnancy. They educate them regarding the different options available to them. Usually, the options include, parenting, adoption and abortion. Therefore, pregnancy options counseling is highly useful in guiding women in taking a right decision regarding how they should proceed with their pregnancy.

Abortion

Prevalence

One option that a woman with an unplanned pregnancy may consider is abortion, the deliberate termination of a pregnancy. According to the World Health Organization (WHO), about 40–50 million abortions are performed worldwide each year. About 20 million of these abortions are considered unsafe and result in around 67,000 deaths each year. Abortion rates are similar across countries despite its being legal in some and illegal in others. In other words, just as many women get abortions in countries where it is illegal as in countries where it is legal. The only difference is that they proceed with illegal abortions, which are more likely to be provided under unsafe conditions by poorly trained providers. A woman's pregnancy options in regards to abortion would be presented differently by her counselor, depending on the country they are in. The Mexico City Policy is an example of governments restricting this aspect of pregnancy options counseling.

Worldwide Abortion Policies

Different countries have different abortion policies, which are based on the extent to which the unplanned pregnancy is affecting mother and fetus. 96 percent of countries allow abortions to save a woman whose life is at risk. Six countries in the world do not permit the termination of a pregnancy under any circumstance; that is 3% of the world's countries that don't allow abortion at all. There are 50 countries (26%) that allow an abortion only if it is to save the mother's life, 82 countries (42%) that allow abortion to save the mother's life or for at least one of the following reasons: to preserve the woman's physical health, to preserve the woman's mental health, in the case of rape or incest, to avoid fetal impairment, or for economic or social reasons. Lastly, 58 countries (30%) allow abortions on request for any reason, though these countries usually do not allow the pregnancy to be terminated beyond a certain stage.

Types of Abortion

Should a pregnant woman's country allow her to get an abortion, a pregnancy counselor can help her to address the tough questions that might arise and give her information on the types of abortion. Once a woman has decided on abortion, there are two ways in which one can be induced. The first type of abortion is a medical abortion that involves the use of drugs. This option is only feasible within the first 9 weeks of pregnancy. After that, the only other option is a surgical abortion, which involves the removal of the placenta and fetus.

Adoption

Adoption is a permanent, legal transfer of parental rights and responsibilities from child's birth parents to the adoptive parents. Pregnant women looking to place their child up for adoption have many options as to how much involvement they wish to have in choosing the adoptive parents and to some degree. Nonetheless, birthmothers choosing to put their child up for adoption are legally terminating their parental rights to the child. Adoption laws differ state by state; adoption agencies, counselors, and lawyers can be used to provide information to the birth parents and adoptive parents about this process.

Types of Adoption

There are two general types of adoption to choose from: closed adoption, and open adoption. Closed adoptions are when the birthmother and adoptive parents have no contact with one another. In this case, the records of the biological parents are kept sealed. Closed adoptions are becoming less common within the United States but are still prevalent in international adoptions. Open adoptions occur when the biological mother and adoptive parents chose to keep in touch, though the amount and type of contact varies case by case, depending on what both parties agree on.

Choosing to Parent

Prenatal Care

If a pregnant woman seeking pregnancy options counseling is considering completing her pregnancy, whether it be in the case of adoption or that she is choosing to parent, her next step would be to start prenatal care. Prenatal care is a type of preventative healthcare, which serves to prevent potential health problems and promote a healthy lifestyle during the pregnancy.

Lifestyle Changes

If a mother choses to parent her child, she should also expect to make some lifestyle changes to ensure the health and safety of her unborn child. The suggested lifestyle changes include stopping the consumption of caffeine, alcohol, cigarettes, marijuana, recreational drugs, and prescription drugs. The mother is also encouraged to have a healthy diet and excursive regularly.

Pre-conception Counseling

Preconception counseling is defined as health education and promotion. The goal of preconception care is health education and promotion, risk assessment, and intervention before pregnancy to reduce chances of poor perinatal outcomes. Nearly half of the 200 million pregnancies that occur annually are unplanned. Preconception counseling can play a major role in reducing poor perinatal outcomes. Preconception counseling targeted at the mother, father, and family can reduce maternal and infant morbidity and mortality. Preconception counseling and education must include early health promotion and information to guide families in identifying risks and addressing those risks before pregnancy.

Issues of Concern

In anticipation of future childbearing years, every individual benefits from education about pregnancy readiness and the role of family and parenting with age appropriate education. As children enter puberty, both boys and girls must be educated about the delay in sexuality, pregnancy prevention, and prevention of sexually transmitted infections. Although education may not correlate with delayed sexual activity, it is important to educate young males about their responsibilities in reproductive health. Every couple must have the opportunity to choose when they are ready to reproduce. Family planning and pregnancy prevention is key to pregnancy readiness. Unplanned and unintended pregnancy results in late prenatal care which can subsequently contribute to adverse events during pregnancy and poor perinatal outcomes. Both the woman and man must be assessed for risks and educated about the risks associated with poor perinatal outcomes. This risk assessment must include evaluation of overall well-being, medical history, surgical risks, social and behavioral risks, medication risks, occupational risks, education risks, and any other barriers that may pose an undue risk on fertility or pregnancy. A few important items to discuss during preconception counseling include:

Management of Chronic Disease

Any woman with a chronic disease should review her desire to become pregnant with the primary care physician or provider and her family. Pregnancy can increase risks for both the mother and the child requiring additional visits, changes in routine care, and possible prolonged hospital stays if the perinatal period and pregnancy outcomes are not optimal. Preconception counseling must focus on optimizing both primary and secondary prevention, treatment compliance, and improving overall well-being prior to becoming pregnant. Any identified risks including disease history and status, current medications, social barriers, and limited support systems or financial barriers must also be reviewed. Patients with diseases or health issues associated with progression during pregnancy such as severe depression and anxiety, seizure disorders, diabetes, cardiac, renal disease, and other long-term illnesses should be referred for further counseling with a high-risk provider to discuss possible changes in medical management during pregnancy.

Genetic Disorders and Carrier States

Families with histories of genetic disorders should be referred to a genetic counselor to discuss the risks of passing the disorder to the newborn. The genetic counselor can also educate the family on disorders that might impact fertility.

Folic Acid

Early use of Folic acid prevents neural tube defects. Women of reproductive age should be prescribed folic acid during the preconception period and throughout pregnancy. (Level A)

Short Interval Pregnancy (Less Than 18 Months)

Short interval pregnancies are associated with preterm deliveries, premature rupture of membranes, maternal morbidity, and mortality, third trimester bleeding, myometritis, and anemia. Counseling about short interval pregnancy and the negative impact would likely reduce the number of short interval pregnancies (Level B).

Smoking Cessation

Tobacco use is associated with preterm labor, intrauterine growth retardation, low birth weight, and placental abruption. Smoking cessation can reduce perinatal mortality and low birth weight by at least 20%. Smoking cessation should be offered to the woman and her partner before and during early pregnancy (Level A). Women should be counseled that secondhand smoke can impact both fertility and the perinatal period.

Alcohol Use

Alcohol use in pregnancy is associated with fetal alcohol syndrome and fertility problems. Women should be advised to avoid alcohol if they are planning a pregnancy.

Obesity

Obesity is associated with multiple perinatal risks including increased risk for gestational diabetes, hypertension, congenital heart diseases in the fetus, and a higher risk of difficult deliveries, cesarean section, and complications of delivery. Women with a BMI > 40 should be counseled to see a dietician. Women who are obese have higher risks for chronic diseases such as hypertension, diabetes mellitus, heart disease, and stroke all of which can lead to additional complications in pregnancy. Obesity is an independent risk factor in pregnancy with a higher chance of developing pregnancy-associated hypertension, insulin-dependent gestational diabetes, and macrosomic infants.

Underweight

Women with malnutrition may be at risk for nutrient deficiencies that increase the risk for low birth weight in the fetus and preterm labor.

Substance Use

Use of drugs in pregnancy is associated with neonatal abstinence syndrome, placental abruption (cocaine), low birth weight, maternal morbidity such as hemorrhage, and fetal and infant mortality. Women should be advised to discontinue use of substances. Education must include both perinatal risk and risk to mother and neonate long-term.

Toxin Exposure

Women should be counseled to avoid toxic substances (Level C). Toxins with potential impact to reproductive health include lead, arsenic, fluoride, toluene, flame retardants, plastics, and pesticides.

Environmental Exposures

Preconception assessment of home environment, community, and occupational hazards are important to recognizing and reducing potential risks during pregnancy especially during the organogenesis period. The assessment must include exposure history and duration of exposure. Education and counseling must include the warnings of birth defects and potential transmission of toxins in breastfeeding. Exposure to chemicals in the community and work environment may be linked to birth defects, fetal loss, and low fertility. Couples should be encouraged to inquire about potential hazards in the workplace.

Medication Exposures

Preconception counseling must include careful evaluation of medications taken by the women prior to pregnancy. Allowing adequate time for the transition to less harmful medicines and optimizing dosing can lead to both improved perinatal outcomes and avoidance of anomalies and poor outcomes for the fetus.

Diabetes Management

Uncontrolled diabetes is associated with congenital heart defects, intrauterine growth retardation, and miscarriage. In the neonate, it can be associated with hypoglycemia, respiratory distress syndrome, hyperbilirubinemia. For the mother, it is associated with increased risk of hypertension, visual problems, and infections. Women, who can maintain A1C level less than 7, will have a lower risk of complications including congenital heart defects (Level A). Counseling during the preconception period must focus on disease management and education, optimal control, weight management, and education about the potential risks to mother and fetus during the perinatal period.

Infectious Diseases Management

Couples should receive counseling about treatment and potential risks to the mother and baby. Infections with known adverse effects or long-term sequelae in the perinatal period are listed below.

- Hepatitis B - Preconception counseling should include a review of a risk factor for hepatitis B and any history of treatment of a prior diagnosis of the virus. Literature supports vaccinating women who are at high risk for hepatitis B during the preconception period. Women with positive hepatitis B status must be educated about risks to the newborn and associated risks of hepatocellular carcinoma for chronic hepatitis B carriers.

- Human Immunodeficiency Virus (HIV) - Prior to pregnancy, parents should be evaluated for risk of HIV and those with known positivity must be treated. Women at high risk for HIV should be counseled on prevention and guided on the risk of transmission to the newborn if they should become positive during pregnancy. Those with known HIV status must be educated about the risk of transmission, educated about the reduction in transmission with proper treatment, and encouraged to adhere to medical management throughout the pregnancy. Proper treatment of HIV during pregnancy can reduce transmission as much as 75 percent (Level A).
- Tetanus - The World Health Organization recommends that all women of childbearing age be protected against tetanus. The mortality rate of tetanus is as high as 1 in 10 people when Tetanus is diagnosed. Women at high risk should be vaccinated prior to pregnancy. It is safe to administer tetanus vaccine (Td) during pregnancy in any trimester. It is standard practice in the United States to administer tetanus vaccine along with pertussis (Tdap) between 27 and 36 weeks gestation.
- MMR -Preconception counseling should include a vaccination history that includes measles, mumps, and rubella. These viruses can have moderate to severe effects during pregnancy or increase the risk of miscarriage. It is important to vaccinate before pregnancy if the woman has not been vaccinated. The Centers for Disease Control recommend waiting at least 28 days after receiving rubella containing vaccine before pregnancy.

Preconception counseling must include communication to the potential mother and father. During the preconception counseling, the provider has the opportunity to perform the risk assessment. Risk assessment includes reviewing a thorough history of medical, surgical, psychosocial, genetic, nutrition, and behavioral risks. These include screening for alcohol and drug use. Couples should be reminded about the importance of vaccination for the mother and early access to prenatal care if pregnancy occurs. Women with behavioral health issues should be counseled to see their provider for medication management and changes if needed. Early preconception counseling and intervention has the potential to reduce perinatal morbidity and mortality. Pregnancy readiness and a planned pregnancy is the optimal goal. Families seeking future pregnancies should be counseled to seek primary care to address any identified risks and to discuss pregnancy planning.

References

- Van Esbroeck, R.; Athanansou, J. (2008). "1. Introduction". In Athanasou, J. & R. Van Esbroeck. International Handbook of Career Guidance. Springer. pp. 1–19. ISBN 978-1-4020-6229-2

- Career-counseling, learn-about-therapy: goodtherapy.org, Retrieved 10 July 2018
- Whiston, Susan C.; Li, Yue; Mitts, Nancy Goodrich; Wright, Lauren. "Effectiveness of career choice interventions: A meta-analytic replication and extension". Journal of Vocational Behavior. 100: 175–184. doi:10.1016/j.jvb.2017.03.010
- Career-counselling-meaning-benefits-importance: mindler.com, Retrieved 19 May 2018
- Rosenthal, Elisabeth (12 October 2007). "Legal or Not, Abortion Rates Compare". The New York Times. ISSN 0362-4331. Retrieved 23 March 2017
- What-is-existential-counselling: affinitycentre.co.uk, Retrieved 27 June 2018
- Stone, Gerald L.; Lucas, Julie (Jan–Feb 1994). "Disciplinary Counseling in Higher Education: A Neglected Challenge". Journal of Counseling and Development. 72 (3): 234–38. doi:10.1002/j.1556-6676.1994.tb00927.x
- Grief-counseling: minddisorders.com, Retrieved 09 July 2018
- Paul, Annie Murphy (2004). The Cult of Personality. New York: Free Press (Simon & Schuster). pp. 118–136. ISBN 0-7432-4356-0
- Can-grief-counseling-really-help-what-it-is-and-how-it-works: betterhelp.com, Retrieved 17 May 2018
- Mcilveen, P.; Patton, W. (2007-09-01). "Narrative career counselling: Theory and exemplars of practice". Australian Psychologist. 42 (3): 226–235. doi:10.1080/00050060701405592. ISSN 1742-9544
- Rehabilitation-counseling, counseling-process, counseling-psychology: psychology.iresearchnet.com, Retrieved 17 June 2018

3

Concepts of Counseling

Counseling empowers individuals, families and groups to achieve good mental health, educational, relationship and career goals. The aim of this chapter is to explore the varied concepts of counseling, such as relationship education, academic advising, self-help, emotional conflict, etc.

Relationship Education

Relationship education generally works with couples who are currently satisfied with their relationship and hoping to prevent relationship distress and breakdown through a focus on "building the foundations for a positive life together". Broadly defined, relationship education is:

Efforts or programs that provide education, skills and principles that help individuals (a person not in a relationship or a person without his or her partner) and couples (both partners participating) increase their chances of having healthy and stable relationships.

In Australia more than one third of couples go to *premarital* relationship education before they get married. Relationship education incorporates more programs, and is available in more settings, than these traditional premarital classes. Relationship education is not restricted to engaged couples preparing for marriage, and is not only church-based, although in Australia programs are most commonly offered through religious organizations. Relationship education programs can also be run as part of other programs including antenatal classes, parenting programs, the school curriculum, and rebuilding after separation or divorce programs, in which relationship education material can be embedded. Markman and Rhoades described the types of programs included under the umbrella term "relationship education" as:

- couple enrichment and enhancement programs: typically marital health promotion interventions aimed at helping couples increase their levels of marital satisfaction;
- communication programs: designed to teach couples effective communication skills; and
- prevention programs: which are divided into three groups:
- universal prevention programs: for all couples, usually starting when couples are young and happy, aiming to keep couples happy;
- selective intervention programs: for couples at risk for distress or divorce; and
- Indicated programs: for couples in the early stages of distress.

Marriage and relationship education programs are typically offered to couples in a group setting; however, the couple, or individual, can also direct their own relationship education in what is known as *self-directed* relationship education. Self-help books and DVDs are common forms of self-directed relationship education, and recent developments have seen an increase in the number of self-directed relationship programs available on the Internet.

There are two evidence-based strategies commonly used in relationship education programs that are fairly widely adopted: assessment with feedback and curriculum-based knowledge and skills training.

Assessment with Feedback

Assessment with feedback approaches usually comprises inventory-based couple assessments followed by a feedback session with a relationship educator who informs the couple of their current relationship strengths and weaknesses.

The three most common inventories used in practice are PREmarital Preparation And Relationship Enhancement (PREPARE), the Facilitating Open Couple Communication Understanding and Study (FOCCUS) and RELATionship Evaluation (RELATE).

These inventories share a number of commonalities. Partners complete the inventories independently, and the content of each inventory is similar. Questionnaires are used to score couples across dimensions such as shared realistic relationship expectations, effective communication and conflict resolution skills, and emotional health and effective individual stress management. Computers are used to score the results for all inventories, with each providing the couple with a summary report used to predict couples' future relationship satisfaction and stability.

There are some differences, however. The RELATE questionnaire is more comprehensive and is available online, not requiring any involvement from a relationship educator.

Although these inventory assessments are relatively quick and inexpensive to administer, Halford identified several weaknesses with the research behind the assessment with feedback approach, including the lack of published systematic evaluations of the long-term effects on relationship outcomes and the reliance on couples to self-report their behaviors rather than researchers observing the couples interacting.

Curriculum-based knowledge and Skills Training

Curriculum-based approaches are relationship education programs concentrating on the active training of key relationship skills and place a significant focus on building knowledge.

Some commonly used curriculum-based programs include the Relationship Enhancement (RE) program, the Prevention and Relationship Enhancement Program (PREP), the Couple Commitment and Relationship Enhancement (Couple CARE) program, Couples Communication Program (CCP) and Couples Coping Enhancement Training (CCET).

These programs share many similarities, including a focus on skills training in positive communication, conflict management and positive expression of affection however, they also vary in significant ways, particularly in their emphasis on certain content such as the development of partner empathy in Relationship Enhancement and the development of relationship self-regulation in Couple CARE.

Goals for Couples

Goals of relationship education include helping couples learn to:

- Confide in one another regularly with emotional openness and empathic listening.

In more basic terms, trust one another. Trust is one of the most important building blocks in every healthy relationship. Without it, a relationship can not grow stronger. Feelings should not be kept secret and walls must be broken down when entering a relationship. Being trustworthy with one another brings many positive outcomes for both partners and can also bring the couple closer to each other. For this reason, trust is something that you do not want to break. In most cases, if trust is lost, it is very difficult to regain. Though it is not impossible, it is best to keep honesty alive and well in a relationship. As long as both partners are completely open and comfortable with each other, trust will be present.

- Complain to one another regularly (without attacking) including requests for change. Can listen to complaints without defensiveness.
- Resolve differences and conflicts by seeking to learn rather than to prevail. Use fair fighting that involves confiding, empathic listening, complaining with requests for change, and contracting, effective win-win solutions, all without manipulation or dirty fighting.
- Agree upon areas of autonomy, areas of consultation, and areas of mutually shared ownership and decision-making.
- Clarify hidden assumptions and unspoken expectations to minimize misperception and misunderstanding.
- Help one another heal pains and disappointments, resolve emotional allergies, and clarify hidden assumptions. Conjointly heal and resolve emotional allergy infinity loops.
- Meet basic needs for sensuality, appropriate sexuality, physical closeness, bonding, and intellectual and emotional sharing with one another.
- Follow clear, equal, negotiated boundaries regarding what is private and not shared with others outside the relationship.
- Initiate change when the status quo (division of roles, responsibilities, and privileges) is not satisfactory. Follow through on negotiated changes.

Examples

The National Council on Family Relations focuses on preparing professionals in family life education, a prominent approach to relationship education.

In 2006, the U.S. Department of Health and Human Services began funding significant multi-year demonstration projects through the Administration for Children and Families to expand the availability of marriage education classes in more than 100 communities nationwide. This project, known as the "Healthy Marriage Initiative," was designed to improve the well-being of children by providing tools and education to strengthen marriages and families.

Jeffry H. Larson conducted several studies on marriage and relationship education, including a review of three widely used premarital inventories - Focus, Prepare, and Relate.

Seven Principles of Relationship Education

1. It's Your Ship, You're the Captain: Relationship education is about helping people find strategies and solutions that fit for their unique circumstances, values and relationship goals. That includes respecting their own personal responsibility for their success and the decisions they make for their lives. Evidence-based skills training provides techniques that are easy to understand and use to surface greater awareness of what lies beneath the tip of the iceberg, navigate typical relationship challenges, and overcome differences that are a natural part of any close relationship.

2. One Mouth, Two Ears: Relationship education provides safe, time-limited structures for conversations that matter, which are often much more about listening than talking. Learning to actively listen with empathy and respect to another person's perspective and experience –without judgment, defensiveness, blame, or an effort to quickly try to "fix" the issue or the person — makes it safer for intimates to develop greater awareness of themselves and each other.

3. Riding the Waves: Relationship education teaches practical, usable skills for better understanding and safely expressing the full range of emotions, including anger, sadness and fear. Upsetting feelings held in eventually either implode or explode. Confiding painful feelings to a significant other leaves more room to experience feelings of love, pleasure and happiness. Just as the most powerful waves lose their energy when they break against the shore, the same is generally true of emotions.

4. It's Rarely the Problem that's the Problem: Relationship education enables distressed couples — with good will towards each other, openness to learning, and a desire for the relationship to succeed — to deal with differences and problems in ways that often lead to greater closeness, understanding, acceptance and commitment. The issues that surface are typically symptoms of communication breakdowns, hidden assumptions and expectations, behaviors that come from holding in upsetting feelings, or lack of skills for constructive conflict resolution.

5. Love is a Feeling: Relationship education helps people develop their emotional intelligence, including understanding that feelings of love come from the anticipation of pleasure in our interactions with others. If instead of anticipating pleasure, we expect pain, feelings of love are unlikely to survive, let alone thrive. What's a pleasure changes during different stages and passages of life. Sustaining feelings of love requires learning what it takes in today's circumstances to stay a pleasure in each other's lives. And doing it.

6. Marriage is a Contract: Relationship education recognizes that although nearly all traditional marriage vows include the promise to "love 'till death do us part," the marriage contract itself cannot be dependent on "feelings" of love, which naturally wax and wane. That doesn't mean commitment or obligations wax and wane. Emotions are affected by many factors, often unrelated to issues inside our closest relationships.

Marriage is the glue that's meant to hold couples and families together during periods of growth, change and challenge that are natural part of life.

7. Relationships are Work: Relationship education is built on the understanding that what happens in our closest relationships impacts quality of life, fulfillment, happiness, and the ability to pursue cherished dreams and aspirations. Relationships take regular attention. Without intentionally nurturing relationships, it's easy to become strangers, for relationships to wither and become vulnerable. Beyond staying a pleasure in each other's lives, the work of an intimate relationship is to consistently meet each other's needs for bonding (emotional and physical closeness). Relationship education provides a road map and usable skills for sustaining healthy relationships that are an ongoing source of love, pleasure, happiness, and fulfillment for both partners.

Qualities of Effective Relationship Educators

PAIRS Foundation defines the qualities of effective relationship educators to include:

Personal Qualities

- Warmth, optimism, authenticity, poise, and maturity
- Emotionally stable and comfortable with emotional intensity
- Appropriate professional appearance and grooming
- At ease with groups
- Asks for help when needed

Presentation Qualities

- Fully prepared for each class with clear, organized presentations
- Speaks clearly with appropriate pacing, expression, and is easily understood
- Relevant and appropriate self-disclosure
- Avoids wordiness, professional jargon, terminology
- Use of appropriate humor
- Establishes group rapport
- Avoids inappropriate comments or offensive behavior
- Knowledge of the curriculum and its intended purpose
- Provides clear and accurate direction
- Stays within boundaries and topics of each class

- Effectively teaches evidence-based curriculum content as it is written
- Covers all required material and exercises within time allowed
- Handles transitions effectively
- Appropriately evaluates and reads participant responses
- Receives positive evaluations from class participants

Presenting as a Couple or Team

- Works cooperatively with staff and team members
- Authentically models curriculum tools and values

Ethical Practices

- Knowledge, understanding, and adherence to Ethical practices
- Understands and respects the vulnerabilities of class participants
- Ability to maintain a safe educational environment, including appropriate boundaries

Relationship Education for Veterans

The Veterans Health Administration announced a nationwide relationship education initiative for Veterans in October 2012. The program, known as "Warriors to Soul Mates," is based on a curriculum developed by PAIRS Foundation. "The Department of Veterans Affairs has a new goal to care for and heal our wounded Veterans. In addition to repairing their damaged bodies and minds, VA has embarked on a unique campaign to repair their crumbling intimate relationships."

Relationship Education for Premarital Couples

A multi-year federal study, known as the Building Strong Families Program, and 2010 meta-analysis of 47 studies found that relationship education "does not improve relationship quality/satisfaction" for unmarried couples.

"Previous studies have asserted that premarital education programs have a positive effect on program participants. Using meta-analytic methods of current best practices to look across the entire body of published and unpublished evaluation research on premarital education, we found a more complex pattern of results. We coded 47 studies and found that premarital education programs do not improve relationship quality/satisfaction when unpublished studies are included in the analysis, although studies that follow couples past the honeymoon stage to detect prevention effects are rare. In contrast, premarital education programs appear to be effective at improving couple communication, with studies that employed observational measures rather than self-report measures producing large effects. Still, given the mixed, modest results, there is ample room and a real need to improve the practice of premarital education."

Building Strong Families Program

Between 2002 and 2011, Mathematica Policy Research conducted the Building Strong Families Program study for the U.S. Department of Health and Human Services, Administration for Children and Families, "to learn whether well-designed interventions can help couples fulfill their aspirations for a healthy relationship, marriage, and a strong family."

The study specifically evaluated the impact of relationship education classes delivered to more than 5,000 low-income, unwed couples at 12 locations in seven states. "The intervention featured up to 42 hours of multi-couple group sessions led by trained facilitators, focusing on skills that, according to earlier research, are associated with relationship and marital stability and satisfaction."

In May 2010, Mathematica reported findings from a 15-month follow-up of program and control group participants:

- BSF had no effect on whether couples were still together 15 months after they had applied for the program, when data from the eight BSF programs are combined. At this point, 76 percent of BSF couples were still romantically involved, compared with 77 percent of control group couples. Similarly, BSF and control group couples were equally likely to be married to each other at that time (17 and 18 percent respectively) and to be living together, whether married or unmarried (62 percent for both research groups)."
- Fifteen months after they applied for the program, BSF and control group couples reported being equally happy in their romantic relationships, with average ratings of 8.4 and 8.3 respectively on a 0-to-10 relationship happiness scale. Similarly, BSF and control group couples gave very similar ratings of supportiveness and affection in their relationships, with average support and affection scale values of 3.5 on a 1-to-4 scale for couples in both research groups. In addition, BSF had no overall effect on how faithful couples were to each other.
- When results are averaged across all eight programs, BSF did not improve couples' ability to manage their conflict. Couples in both research groups reported similar levels of use of constructive conflict behaviors, such as keeping a sense of humor and listening to the other partner's perspective during disagreements. Similarly, there was no difference between the research groups in the avoidance of destructive conflict behaviors, such as withdrawing when there is a disagreement or allowing small disagreements to escalate. In addition, when results are averaged across all programs, BSF had no effect on how likely couples were

to experience intimate partner violence. Similarly, when results are averaged across all programs, BSF did not improve co-parenting or increase father involvement. BSF and control group couples reported that their co-parenting relationships were of equally high quality. In addition, at the 15-month follow-up, couples in both research groups were equally likely to report that fathers were living with their children, spending substantial time with them, and providing them with substantial financial support.

- The Baltimore BSF program [Loving Couples, Loving Children] had negative effects on couples' relationships. BSF couples were less likely than control group couples to remain romantically involved, 59 percent versus 70 percent. Baltimore BSF couples reported being less supportive and affectionate toward each other than control group couples did. In addition, women in the Baltimore BSF program were more likely than women in the control group to report having been severely physically assaulted by a romantic partner in the past year, 15 percent compared with 9 percent. Baltimore BSF couples also rated the quality of their co-parenting relationship lower than control group couples did and reported that BSF fathers spent less time with their children and were less likely to provide them financial support than control group fathers were.

Relationship Education for Married Couples

Several studies, notably the Supporting Healthy Marriage Project funded by the U.S. Department of Health and Human Services, Administration for Children and Families, a meta-analysis by Hawkins and Ooms and a five-year impact report by Peluso, Eisenberg and Schindler found that relationship education provided statistically significant benefits for married couples.

"The emerging evidence suggests that MRE [marriage and relationship education] programs can work for low-income populations as well as for those who are economically better off. The evidence from a new meta-analysis of 15 program evaluations (including three randomized control trials) shows that MRE programs can have positive, moderate size effects on low-income couples' relationship outcomes, at least in the short run. However, the largest and most rigorous study of low-income, unmarried couples produced mixed results and shows there is still much to learn. MRE improves communication—a core, essential relationship skill—as well as other measures of relationship quality. There is also some initial evidence that MRE for low-income couples can decrease divorce rates, reduce aggression, and improve children's problem behaviors.

Supporting Healthy Marriage Study

In August 2012, Manpower Development Research Corporation (MDRC), a nonprofit, nonpartisan social policy research organization, reported that a federally funded, multi-year, random assignment, control group study known as the Supporting Healthy Marriage Project found high levels of consumer satisfaction among 4,989 adults participating in relationship education courses based on the work of PREP Inc., PAIRS Foundation and John Gottman at sites in Florida (Orlando), Kansas (Wichita), Pennsylvania (Reading and Bethlehem), Texas (El Paso and San Antonio), New York (Bronx), Oklahoma (Oklahoma City), and Washington (Shoreline and Seattle). A 12-month report on the program's impact found:

Couple practices communication skills during PAIRS Foundation relationship education class in Florida.

- The SHM program produced a consistent pattern of small positive effects on multiple aspects of couples' relationships. Relative to the control group, the program group showed higher levels of marital happiness, lower levels of marital distress, greater warmth and support, more positive communication, and fewer negative behaviors and emotions in their interactions with their spouses. The consistency of results across outcomes and data sources (surveys and independent observations of couple interactions) is noteworthy.
- Compared with individuals in the control group, program group members reported experiencing slightly less psychological and physical abuse from their spouses. Men and women in the program group reported less psychological abuse in their relationships, and men in the program group reported that their spouses physically assaulted them less often, compared with their control group counterparts.
- Men and women in the program group reported slightly lower levels of adult psychological distress (such as feelings of sadness or anxiety) than their control group counterparts.
- The program did not significantly affect whether couples stayed married at the 12-month follow-up point.

Academic Advising

Academic advising is a decision-making process by which students realize their maximum educational potential through communication and information exchanges with an advisor. It is ongoing, multifaceted, and the responsibility of both the student and the advisor.

Although advising is a shared responsibility between an advisor and the student, it is ultimately the student's responsibility to make decisions about their life goals by creating a plan to reach those goals. The advisor serves as a facilitator of communication and a coordinator of learning experiences through course and career planning and academic progress reviews. It's a student-centered process that enables one to make the most of their university experience.

Academic advisors are committed to providing every undergraduate student with high-quality assistance, in order to support them in the development and pursuit of academic objectives consistent with their life goals and the available opportunities.

Standards

Of significance to the profession of academic advising are the Standards and Guidelines for Academic Advising that have been developed by the Council for the Advancement of Standards in Higher Education (CAS) and endorsed by the National Academic Advising Association (NACADA). These Standards and Guidelines are available at the NACADA web site. The Standards and their accompanying Guidelines cover thirteen areas from Mission to Assessment. The current Standards and Guidelines were last updated in 2005.

Models

A variety of approaches exist to academic advising, each of which is informed by the goals of the advisor-student interaction. Three principle models of advising include developmental advising, prescriptive advising, and intrusive advising.

Developmental Advising

Developmental advising was first introduced by Crookson in 1972. This approach is focused on helping students explore and define academic, career and life goals and pathways, and develop problem-solving and decision-making skills through collaborative and process-oriented advising. Fostering a relationship between the advisor and student is critical to this model, which is based primarily on adult development theory and student development theory. Although many studies have shown that students generally prefer this approach it can require a greater commitment of time and resources compared to other advising models.

Prescriptive Advising

The prescriptive or traditional advising model is focused primarily on providing students with information directly related to their academic program and progress, such as academic policies, major/program requirements and course selection. Prescriptive advising is normally initiated by the student as the goal of this approach is to address immediate questions to facilitate the student's progress through their academic program, rather than play a role in helping the student form long-term goals beyond their academic pursuits. This type of advising is sometimes equated to a doctor-patient relationship model.

Intrusive Advising

A model for intrusive advising (also known as high involvement or proactive advising) was first introduced by Glennon in 1975. A defining feature of this approach is that contact is initiated by the advisor rather than the student. Generally, contact with students is initiated at critical periods throughout a student's academic career, such as during a student's first year of study, while taking developmental or remedial courses, before they must declare a major, or as they approach graduation. Additionally, particular cohorts of students may be targeted such as academically at-risk students (e.g. students on probation), or high-achieving students. In practice intrusive advising has been shown to have a positive impact on developmental/remedial undergraduate mathematics course pass rates, as well as student retention and degree attainment rates, and research indicates that students prefer this approach to advising over strictly prescriptive advising. However, it is important to note that some students may find this approach invasive.

Misc Advising

Advising has been around for sometime, but there are many different settings of advising. The differences can include from high school to undergraduate degrees to graduate degrees. In research it is shown that there are two specific colleges advising that have been helpful to students asking for advice. Collaborative and individualistic are those two. Individualistic is similar to intrusive and is not necessary to repeat information. Collaborative advising is shown to be more helpful than individualistic advising and has been shown to help due to the group participation. Students learn more from other students co-advising them. They learn more when details become more realistic and generalizable. Collaborative advising is also where group advisors and group advisees work together to come up with multiple solutions to give the students' options.

Effectiveness

Academic advising is shown to be more successful when advisors hold face-to-face appointments with their advisees. Particularly with topics like future classes, and careers. Face-to-face interactions make advising more meaningful for the students. Additionally, students place more importance on the supportive and caring nature of their relationship with their advisor than on the particular approach to advising.

Participation in academic advising has been shown to increase student satisfaction and mitigate students' feelings of isolation or disconnection from the institution as a whole are linked to with increased university student retention and graduation rates, and reduced attrition and withdrawal rates. This effect has been documented for both traditional 'on-campus' institution and institutions, which offer courses and/or entire programs through online/virtual formats.

Academic advisors assist in the process of academic advising by helping one understand one's options, determine resources and, when necessary, identify alternatives.

The advisor's role is an active rather than a passive one and the process of advising requires the following objectives to be met for each student assigned as an advisee:

- Help students define and develop realistic educational career plans through schedule planning for each semester and summer school, if appropriate. Each student should have an up-to-date academic schedule plan through to graduation.
- (Freshmen advisees) Meet with advisee during orientation to assist student with initial adjustment to university academic life. Special sessions should be scheduled throughout the first academic year.
- (For continuing advisees) Meet at least once each semester with continuing students to plan for the coming semester (or summer) and to review/revise long range academic program schedules.
- Assist students in planning a program consistent with their abilities and interests.
- Monitor progress toward educational/career goals and meet at least once each

semester to review the progress toward completing the proposed academic program and to discuss grades and other performance indicators.

- Discuss and reinforce linkages and relationships between instructional program and occupation/career.
- Interpret and provide rationale for institutional policies, procedures, and requirements.
- Follow-up with the advisee on any report of unsatisfactory work (notice of class probation for poor attendance, notice of FA and/or failing grades, incomplete grades from past semester(s), etc.). Special attention should be paid to students who are placed on academic probation.
- Approve all designated educational transactions (e.g., pre-registration/registration schedule, drops/adds, withdrawals, change of major and advisor, waivers, graduation requirements, etc.).
- Try to make informal out-of-class/office contacts to underscore personal interest in the student as an individual.
- Maintain an up-to-date Advising Portfolio, with a summary record of performance to date (grade reports, transcript, requirements completed, etc.), dates of conferences, notation of special circumstances, up-to-date MyStuff information and details, etc.
- Inform and, if necessary, refer students to other institutional resources when academic, attitudinal, attendance, or other personal problems require intervention by other professionals. (e.g., Office of Academic Development, Academic Services, Personal Counseling, etc.)
- Proactively contact and be available for student advisees on a regular basis. Office hours should be posted on the advisor's office door and preferably given to the advisee early in the semester. Advisors should plan for extended hours during pre-registration advising.
- Consult regularly with faculty colleagues in order to have up-to-date information. For career and graduate school options, advisors should refer advisees to the Career Development Center when more information is needed.

Responsibility Assumption

Responsibility assumption is a doctrine stating that an individual is assumed to be substantially or totally responsible for all the circumstances and events that befall him in his personal life, to a much greater extent than is normally thought. The strong believers of responsibility assumption believe that whatever the situation is, it is caused just because of the individual's fault, and it is his past choices or desires which must have led him to that outcome.

Variations in Degree of Personal Responsibility Postulated

The main variable within various interpretations of the responsibility assumption doctrine is the degree to which the individual is considered the cause of his or her own experience, ranging from partial but substantial to total responsibility.

Partial but Substantial Responsibility

In its forms positing less than total responsibility, the doctrine appears in nearly all motivational programs, some psychotherapy, and large group awareness training programs. In programs as non-controversial as books on the power of positive thinking, it functions as a mechanism to point out that each individual does affect the perceived world by the decisions they make each day and by the choices they made in the past. These less absolute forms may be expressed within the rubric that we cannot control the situations that befall us, but we can at least control our attitudes toward them.

Total Responsibility

In its more absolute form, the doctrine becomes both more pronounced and more controversial. Perhaps the most prominent dividing line of controversy is the threshold of reversed mental causation, where sufficient responsibility is assigned to the individual that their thoughts or mental attitudes are considered the actual cause of external situations or physical occurrences rather than vice versa, along the lines of the catchphrase, "mind over matter". Detractors of this absolutist interpretation view this as victim blaming, whereas proponents view it as victim-empowering.

Self-Help

Self-help, also known as self-improvement, is a self-guided economic, emotional or intellectual improvement, based upon some substantial psychological basis. There are different kind of self-help group programs, all having their own unique focus, beliefs, goals, and techniques. The terms, such as, recovery, codependency, and dysfunctional families have become deeply integrated in the self-help culture. Many-a-times, self-help utilizes the information, which is publicly available on Internet and support groups. Self-help groups benefit individuals by building in them emotional support, experiential knowledge, and a sense of belonging. Self-help groups, which are associated with health conditions, may consist of patients and caregivers.

Market

Within the context of the market, group and corporate attempts to aid the "seeker" have moved into the "self-help" marketplace, with Large Group Awareness Trainings, LGATs and psychotherapy systems represented. These offer more-or-less prepackaged solutions to instruct people seeking their own individual betterment, just as "the literature of self-improvement directs the reader to familiar frameworks that the French *fin de siècle* social theorist Gabriel Tarde called 'the grooves of borrowed thought'."

Statistics

At the start of the 21st century, "the self-improvement industry, inclusive of books, seminars, audio and video products, and personal coaching, [was] said to constitute a 2.48-billion dollars-a-year industry" in the United States alone. By 2006, research firm Market data estimated the "self-improvement" market in the U.S. as worth more than $9 billion—including infomercials, mail-order catalogs, holistic institutes, books, audio cassettes, motivation-speaker seminars, the personal coaching market, weight-loss and stress-management programs. Market data projected that the total market size would grow to over $11 billion by 2008. In 2012 Laura Vanderkam wrote of a turnover of 12 billion dollars. In 2013 Kathryn Schulz examined "an $11 billion industry".

Self-help and Professional Service Delivery

Self-help and mutual-help are very different from—though they may complement—service delivery by professionals: note for example the interface between local self-help and International Aid's service delivery model.

Conflicts can and do arise on that interface, however, with some professionals considering that "the twelve-step approach encourages a kind of contemporary version of 19th-century amateurism or enthusiasm in which self-examination and very general social observations are enough to draw rather large conclusions."

The rise of self-help culture has inevitably led to boundary disputes with other approaches and disciplines. Some would object to their classification as "self-help" literature, as with "Deborah Tannen's denial of the self-help role of her books" so as to maintain her academic credibility, aware of the danger that "writing a book that becomes a popular success all but ensures that one's work will lose its long-term legitimacy."

Placebo effects can never be wholly discounted. Thus careful studies of "the power of subliminal self-help tapes showed that their content had no real effect. But that's not what the participants thought." "If they thought they'd listened to a self-esteem tape (even though half the labels were wrong), they felt that their self-esteem had gone up. No wonder people keep buying subliminal tape: even though the tapes don't work, people think they do." One might then see much of the self-help industry as part of the "skin trades. People need haircuts, massage, dentistry, wigs and glasses, sociology and surgery, as well as love and advice."—a skin trade, "not a profession and a science "Its practitioners would thus be functioning as "part of the personal service industry rather than as mental health professionals." While "there is no proof that twelve-step programs 'are superior to any other intervention in reducing alcohol dependence or alcohol-related problems'," at the same time it is clear that "there is something about 'groupishness' itself which is curative." Thus for example "smoking increases mortality risk by a factor of just 1.6, while social isolation does so by a factor of 2.0 suggesting an added value to self-help groups such as Alcoholics Anonymous as surrogate communities."

Some psychologists advocate a positive psychology, and explicitly embrace an empirical self-help philosophy; "the role of positive psychology is to become a bridge between the ivory tower and the main street—between the rigor of academe and the fun of the self-help movement." They aim to refine the self-improvement field by way of an intentional increase in scientifically sound research and well-engineered models. The division of focus and methodologies has produced several subfields, in particular: general positive psychology, focusing primarily on the study of psychological phenomenon and effects; and personal effectiveness, focusing primarily on analysis, design and implementation of qualitative personal growth. This includes the intentional training of new patterns of thought and feeling. As business strategy communicator Don Tapscott puts it, "The design industry is something done to us. I'm proposing we each become designers. But I suppose 'I love the way she thinks' could take on new meaning."

Both self-talk, the propensity to engage in verbal or mental self-directed conversation and thought, and social support can be used as instruments of self-improvement, often by empowering, action-promoting messages. Psychologists have designed series of experiments that are intended to shed light into how self-talk can result in self-improvement. In general, research has shown that people prefer to use second person pronouns over first person pronouns when engaging in self-talk to achieve goals, regulate one's own behavior, thoughts, or emotions, and facilitate performance. If self-talk has the expected effect, then writing about personal problems using language from their friends' perspective should result in greater amount of motivational and emotional benefits comparing to using language from their own perspective. When you need to finish a difficult task and you are not willing to do something to finish this task, trying to write a few sentence or goals imaging what your friends have told you gives you more motivational resources comparing to you write to yourself. Research done by Ireland and others have revealed that, as expected, when people are writing using many physical and mental words or even typing a standard prompt with these kinds of words, adopting a friend's perspective while freely writing about a personal challenge can help increase people's intention to improve self-control by promoting the positivity of emotions such as pride and satisfaction, which can motivate people to reach their goal.

The use of self-talk goes beyond the scope of self-improvement for performing certain activities, self-talk as a linguistic form of self-help also plays a very important role in regulating people's emotions under social stress. First of all, people using non-first-person language tend to exhibit higher level of visual self-distancing during the process of introspection, indicating that using non-first-person pronouns and one's own name may result in enhanced self-distancing. More importantly, this specific form of self-help also has been found can enhance people's ability to regulate their thoughts, feelings, and behavior under social stress, which would lead them to appraise social-anxiety-provoking events in more challenging and less threatening terms. Additionally, these self-help behaviors also demonstrate noticeable self-regulatory effects through the process of social interactions, regardless of their dispositional vulnerability to social anxiety.

Emotional Conflict

An emotional conflict shows an interior knot which is discomfort and that the person must resolve. It is a mess that produces a point of blocking either professionally or on a personal level. Emotional conflicts can be more difficult to identify as they are intangible, i.e., they are not seen in a visible way, however, if they feel. In fact, emotional conflicts feel internally still more the more time passes unless they are resolved. People can turn their backs on their emotional conflicts trying to stay occupied with other issues, however, late or early it emerge a malaise that has not been resolved and that is still there.

Emotional conflicts are directly related to emotional health because there are emotional difficulties that the patient may require appropriate psychological support to face the difficulty.

Conflicts are inevitable, however, when the person feels overwhelmed by a build up of pending Affairs can feel exhausted and discouraged.

Workplace and Emotional Conflict

Everyday dealings, workplace rules, nature of work and interaction with colleagues, customers, and management can all bring about a host of emotions in a person. It is very common for employees to experience emotional conflict at their workplace. Just as a conflict is a situation in which two parties with differing viewpoints are involved, similarly emotional conflict is an intrapersonal situation within an individual during which he feels torn between two or more largely opposing emotions.

For example, during the course of his work, a person might need to take some decisions that go against his values. While this gives him profit at work, it would make him feel a sense of guilt too. Such situations would result in a conflict of emotions- happiness versus doubt and guilt. This has led to the term "working wounded "for employees under such kinds of work situations.

Causes of Emotional Conflict at Work

Emotions run high at workplaces, and it is important to manage these emotions for the wellbeing of employees that in turn lead to the wellbeing of the organization. Following scenarios cause emotional conflict at workplaces:

1. Unfulfilled expectations: When the employee feels under-utilized, sees little or no growth opportunities, does not enjoy his work, or feels that he has to sacrifice his values top sustain his job, he feels demotivated and in a state of conflict with his emotions.

2. Rigid workplace policies: An employee might want the company to move towards newer horizons, contributing substantially towards the society as well, whereas the company would prefer sticking to its original vision and policies.

3. Mismanagement: Miscommunication among employees and leadership causes emotional conflicts the most. When workers' demands are not met, rewards and compensation are not duly given, managers impose unrealistic demands and do not communicate issues properly, it causes a great deal of depression and anxiety among employees and leads to reduced productivity.

Role of Workplace in Resolving Conflicts

If workplace issues remain unresolved, the individual feels restricted at his work. He feels stressed and burned-out. A sense of self-betrayal conflicts with his need for the job to sustain himself. Though it is widely recognized that professional success and emotional conflict go hand in hand, it is in the best interest of the management that they help employees in resolving their workplace emotional conflicts if the company is to function profitably.

1. Leaders should establish an atmosphere of open management and transparency.
2. Equal opportunities must be available to all without biases.
3. Communication is the most important key factor in providing individuals with a sense of reassurance.
4. Companies should not hesitate to avail services of professional advisers and therapists in gaining the trust of employees.

Malan Triangles

Malan's triangle is a schematic way of relating the client's life and relationships in the present and the past and how these impact on the therapeutic relationship in the counseling room. This is a schematic method, whereby we can relate all these ideas and concepts using two triangles.

When people get into conflict (with another person, or inside themselves), they experience a mixture of feelings pulling them in different directions. This can be represented by a Triangle of Conflict. The three points of the triangle are.

Expectations from you

You may be aware of being expected to react in a certain way. What was expected of you from birth onwards? What is expected of you now, and by whom? How do you usually expect yourself to manage life? Who are the key people whose expectations you try to meet? Is this the way you defend yourself from knowing what you truly desire and need?

Your Desires for yourself

Underneath your everyday actions and preoccupations, there are a set of deeply held needs and goals. These might be to do with psychological, physical, relationship or spiritual needs. Do you know what you are seeking out of your life? What are the patterns that prevent you from being fully who you are? What, in this situation, is most important to you? Who would you really like to be?

Your Anxieties and Fears

Your fundamental anxieties are triggered when you move away from what's expected of you towards what you really desire. If you act on your real desires for yourself, will you be abandoned and left alone? Will you lose your mind and go mad in some way? Will you or others be destroyed or die in the process? What are your fears in this situation? What has happened before that makes you fear this happening now? What's stopping you from getting what you need?

References

- Steve Salerno (2005) Sham: How the Self-Help Movement Made America Helpless, ISBN 1-4000-5409-5 pp. 24–25
- Roles-and-responsibilities-of-advisors-and-advisees, general-information, academicadvising: highpoint.edu, Retrieved 09 May 2018
- Drake, J.K. (2011). "The role of academic advising in student retention and persistence". About Campus. 16 (3): 8–12. doi:10.1002/abc.20062
- Starker, Steven (2002). Oracle at the Supermarket: The American Preoccupation With Self-Help Books. Transaction Publishers. p. 62. ISBN 0-7658-0964-8
- What-is-meaning-definition-of-emotional_24: dictionaryofdefinitions.blogspot.com, Retrieved 28 April 2018
- Schulz, Kathryn (2013-01-06). "The Self in Self-Help: We have no idea what a self is. So how can we fix it?". New York Magazine. New York Media, LLC. ISSN 0028-7369. Retrieved 2013-01-11
- Jeschke, M.; Johnson, K.E.; Williams, J.R. (2001). "A Comparison of Intrusive and Prescriptive Advising of Psychology Majors at an Urban Comprehensive University". NACADA Journal. 21 (1/2): 46–58. doi:10.12930/0271-9517-21.1-2.46
- Workplace-and-emotional-conflict: hmworks.n, Retrieved 10 July 2018

- Bitz, Kristi (2013-07-25). "Measuring Advisor Relationship Perceptions Among First-Year Students at a Small Midwestern University". NACADA Journal. 30 (2): 53–64. doi:10.12930/0271-9517-30.2.53
- Gravel, C.A. (2012). "Student-Advisor Interaction in Undergraduate Online Degree Programs: A Factor in Student Retention". NACADA Journal. 32 (2): 56–67. doi:10.12930/0271-9517-32.2.56
- Hidden-Conflict-Malan-s-Triangles-37806584: scribd.com, Retrieved 19 May 2018

4

Counseling Methods

In order to completely understand counseling and counseling methods, it is necessary to study the methodologies of senior peer counseling, online counseling, telephone counseling, suicide prevention, etc. This chapter closely examines these methods for a comprehensive understanding.

Online Counseling

Online therapy, also known as e-therapy, e-counseling, teletherapy or cyber-counseling, is a relatively new development in mental health in which a therapist or counselor provides psychological advice and support over the internet. This can occur through email, video conferencing, online chat, messaging, or internet phone. Online therapy can occur in real-time, such as in phone conversations and online chat rooms, or in a time-delayed format, such as through email messages.

It is important to note that online therapy cannot be considered psychotherapy and will never replace traditional therapy. In many ways, e-therapy shares some similarities with life-coaching. While online therapists cannot diagnose or treat mental illness online, they can offer guidance and advice to people experiencing problems in relationships, work, or life.

E-therapy has limitations, but it is quickly becoming an important resource for a growing number of consumers. Despite a lack of research on the effectiveness of online treatment, e-therapy offers mental health professionals another way of providing services to clients.

Workings of Online Therapy

Primary tools for communicating in online therapy include:

1. Email
2. Instant Messaging (IM)
3. Real-Time Chat
4. Internet Phone
5. Videoconferencing

Distance communication between a therapist and client is not a new concept. Sigmund Freud utilized letters extensively to communicate with his clients. Self-help groups began emerging on the internet as early as 1982. Today, there are numerous sites offering mental health information as well as private e-therapy clinics such as Find-a-Therapist.com.

The growth in online counseling and mental health services has led to the foundation of the International Society for Mental Health Online. This dramatic rise in the availability of online health care has led to a need for information and guidelines for customers interested in receiving mental health services via the internet.

Online Therapy Today

While online therapy is viewed with skepticism by a large number of mental health professionals, it has received support from many patients who have utilized online mental health treatments. In a review of studies published recently, patients receiving mental health treatment through video conferencing reported "high levels of satisfaction."

Online therapy is not appropriate for everyone, but it has shown effectiveness in some situations. For example, recovering addicts might benefit from online therapy, especially for those who feel uncomfortable attending traditional face-to-face support groups.

Before you consider online therapy, you should think about issues such as confidentiality, ethical and legal issues *as well as the qualifications of online therapists.*

Training and Qualifications for Online Therapists

Just as therapists and counselors in "real-world" settings can have a range of qualifications and licenses, online therapists can also differ considerably in their training and credentials. While some sites may promise a quick and easy path to becoming an online therapist, the fact is that the educational and training requirements to become an online therapist are exactly the same as they are for a therapist or counselor practicing in a traditional face-to-face setting.

However, the actual practice of online therapy is very difficult to regulate since therapists can operate from anywhere in the world making it tough to enforce state laws regulating education, training, and scope of practice.

Online therapy is appealing to mental health consumers, who often view it as a convenient, economical and accessible alternative to traditional face-to-face therapy. However, it also poses a number of unique concerns including questions about the confidentiality of client information the appropriateness of using online therapy as a treatment method for various psychological disorders.

If you are interested in becoming an online therapist, then you should check the laws in your state determine the requirements for becoming a licensed therapist or counselor.

The *Online Therapy Institute* also offers a good ethical framework for the use of technology in mental health. These guidelines suggest the minimum practices and standards required for ethical online therapy:

- Therapists should only work within the scope of their practice. In other words, an online therapist should only offer services that he or she is trained to provide.
- Online therapists should adhere to the laws and guidelines specified by their geographic location. For example, in the U.S., only individuals who have received specific training and have passed the required licensing process are legally allowed to call themselves *Psychologists*.
- Therapists should obtain knowledge, training, and supervision in online therapy practices and techniques. This includes formal training (college or university courses), informal training (workshops and conferences), and clinical supervision (either face-to-face or online).
- Online therapists should have a solid understanding of technology. This include both how to use the tools required to deliver psychotherapy online, but also how to ensure that client information remains private and secure.

Problems for which Online Counseling is Provided

Online counseling is provided for a large variety of aspects. Enlisted are just merely a few of them.

Alcoholism	Dysfunctional families	Marriage Problems
Alternative Medicine	Family Issues	Massage Therapy
Anxiety	Family Medicine	Natural Medicine
Career Coaching	Grief Help	Nutritional Advice

Chemical dependence	Healthy relationships	Post-Traumatic Stress Disorder
Chiropractic Questions	Life Transition	Relationship Problems
Codependence	Love addiction	Spiritual Guidance
Depression	Low self-esteem issues	Substance Abuse

Usage of Online Counseling by Students

Online counseling works as a means of constant contact between the students and the counseling center or the counselor. It has proved it's worth time and over again. Online counseling helps in facing, addressing and resolving the distress and challenges faced by students in their life. They are been counseled by licensed professional or a certified counselor. Sincere records of the facts discussed between the student and the counselor are been maintained for future purpose.

Online counseling services have become increasingly popular. Students who are miles away from such assistance – or are not ready to face the spotlight – or the ones who are afraid of being confronted seek help through online counseling. These services are made available 24*7 – 7 days a week and 365 days a year. It also has prescribed policies and procedures for attending and reverting back to students about their anguish. All this comes under the jurisdiction and regulations drawn by the counseling centers or the community college or the alliance for students.

Advantages of Online Counseling for College Students

- Remote and rural students and people can seek assistance for mental health information or distress
- Disabled, household, shy and the ones not ready to come out in public with their problem also can get help
- Fairly affordable and convenient to a large extent
- Easy way of accessing and authenticating the details/resolution shared by the online counselor - re checking the details on internet
- People conveniently talk to family members and friends thru internet applications but are skeptical about discussing mental health; hence online counseling proved to be beneficial in such cases
- Online counseling or e-therapy is a very important aspect to psychological health

Disadvantages of Online Counseling

- No insurance coverage for therapies done through online counseling

- Confidentiality – privacy at stake some times
- Counselors are non reciprocate in emergency circumstances
- Severe psychiatric situation cannot be handled online
- Chances of providing help are less to those ailing from complicated and serious mental health issues
- Facial expressions and body language are not visible to the online counselor to help him understand the severity and authenticity of the student
- Legalities of getting aid strictly from an professional is at stake – anyone can treat anybody in and from any part of the world. However, there are varied requirements for certified and professional counselors for practicing their profession which cannot be counter questioned

Alternatives to Online Counseling

- Attend a support group
- Do nothing at all
- Face to face counseling
- Read a self-help book
- Talk to a friend or family member
- Talk to your doctor
- Telephoning a counseling helpline

Crisis Hotline

Crisis hotline, as its name suggests, is a phone helpline, used in rescuing people in their times of crisis. Through it, people can easily get immediate telephone counseling in the times of emergency. The first crisis hotline kind of service was found in England in 1953. They were initially meant for rescuing those contemplating suicide. But later on, their use got expanded to provide assistance in the times of emotional crisis. Now, such hotlines operate to provide assistance in several other situations and circumstances as well. Some of those circumstances include, helping rape victims, human trafficking victims, runaway children, and people belonging to LGBTQ.

Such services began in 1953, when Chad Varah, an English vicar, founded The Samaritans service, which soon established branches throughout the United Kingdom. The first Samaritans branch in the United States was established in Boston in 1974. In addition to Boston, there are currently Samaritan branches in Falmouth, Massachusetts (serving the Cape Cod and Islands area), the Merrimack Valley, the Fall River/New Bedford area. Outside of Massachusetts, there are branches in New York City, Providence, Hartford, Albany, and Keene, New Hampshire.

In the United States, the Los Angeles Suicide Prevention Center was founded in 1958 and was the first in the country to provide a 24-hour suicide prevention crisis line and use community volunteers in providing hotline service. San Francisco Suicide Prevention started a hotline "Call Bruce" in 1962.

A similar service, Lifeline, was established in Australia in 1963.

Another service, the volunteer-run crisis helpline, Lifelink Samaritans Tas. Inc, originally called Launceston Lifelink, was established in Tasmania in 1968 by concerned citizens of Launceston, Tasmania who decided to create a phone service based on the principles of The Samaritans. The rationale was that people often become suicidal because they cannot discuss their emotional pain with family and friends.

This service provides emotional support 24 hours a day to people throughout Tasmania and does not have any religious affiliations. The organization is a member of Befrienders Worldwide and has a "twinning" relationship with Northampton Samaritans in the UK. Lifelink Samaritans is the oldest telephone befriending service in Tasmania and the fourth oldest in Australia and it receives at least 5,000 calls a year.

Telephone Counseling

Some countries regulate the use of the term "counselor". Telephone counseling and crisis hotlines provide a similar telephone support service, and both usually accept crisis and non-crisis calls. In the United States, many college campuses have established telephone counseling lines serviced by student volunteers to compensate for the high demand placed on college mental health services. These hotlines serve callers in crisis, but also serve to provide a listening ear for people who "just need to talk." Typically, hotlines are staffed by volunteers, and are not intended to replace professional, long-term counseling services. They are rather intended to carry callers through an immediate situation. Such hotlines exist at the University of Maryland, the University of Minnesota, Tufts University, Columbia University, Cornell University, Drexel University, Caldwell University, and Texas A&M University.

Still life

The term "emotional support helpline" is sometimes used – which does not imply crisis or counseling, and can include email and text messaging. Such services have allowed for the wider dissemination of resources for people facing mental health crises.

With developments in mobile telephony, the use of text or SMS (short message service) has been utilized by counseling services. Youthline, a youth-oriented crisis helpline in New Zealand began providing a text messaging counseling support line in 2004

Online, Telephone, TDD/TTY and SMS Help

Examples include:

Hotline/Resource	Organization/Purpose/Focus	Country
1-800-273-TALK (1-800-273-8255) 1-800-SUICIDE (1-800-784-2433)	The National Suicide Prevention Lifeline, a 24/7 hotline for callers in the United States	United States
1-800-799-4TTY (1-800-799-4889)	TTY/TDD services at the National Suicide Prevention Lifeline	United States
1-800-RUNAWAY (1-800-786-2929)	National Runaway Switchboard, hotline and live chat for runaway, homeless, and at-risk youth	United States

800-273-TALK (800-273-8255)	US Veterans Crisis Hotline	United States
veteranscrisisline.net	US Veterans Online chat and information	Worldwide
866-488-7386	An American hotline aimed principally at LGBT teenagers, run by The Trevor Project	United States
1-866-SPEAK-UP (1-866-773-2587)	American anonymous youth violence reporting hotline created by The Center to Prevent Youth Violence	United States
sociedadeamigosdavi-da.org.br	Amigos da Vida (Brazil)	Brazil
The Lowdown	A New Zealand project aimed at young New Zealanders suffering from Depression	New Zealand
1-800-448-3000	The Boys Town National HotlineSM is open 24 hours a day, 365 days a year, and is staffed by specially trained Boys Town counselors.	United States
741-741	A free, 24/7 SMS Hotline providing emotional support for those in crisis provided by Crisis Text Line.	United States
13 11 14	Lifeline offers 24/7 crisis support and suicide prevention services by phone.	Australia

The Volunteer Emotional Support Helplines (VESH) represents 1200 member centers in 61 countries. It has been formed by:

- Befrienders Worldwide (maintained by the Samaritans UK)
- IFOTES – International Federation of Telephone Emergency Services,
- Lifeline International

Telephone Counseling

The telephone has long been considered a professionally acceptable tool for helping counselors provide their services. In the past two decades, there has been an enormous growth in technology aided services provided by psychologists, psychiatrists, social workers and counselors. The use of the telephone has gone beyond answering initial inquiries and scheduling client's appointments to offering full psychological interventions.

Historically, telephone counseling evolved from psychiatric services and medical triage experiences. In the late 1950's crisis hotlines focusing on suicide prevention began to emerge in both Europe and the United States and rapidly expanded to Australia. These hotlines, despite lack of empirical evidence for their effectiveness, soon became part of community mental health services in many places around the world.

The term commonly used is Telehealth or e-health. Telehealth or e-health are terms used to describe any health related service that is provided remotely via technology-assisted media such as the telephone, computer, or Internet. Telepsychology is one form of Telehealth service that is related to remote psychological services. Other terms also commonly used are e-psychology, e-counseling, web-counseling, telephone counseling or online counseling. All of these terms reflect the nature of remote psychological services.

While it is easy to presume that Telepsychology and Helplines provide the same service, there are emerging differences in technology and case management practices that may create distinct differences in the definition of these services. Presently, the difference between Telepsychology and Helplines is in the case management practices of clients. In general terms, Hiplines are community services where people call and talk to someone while remaining anonymous. In the Helpline environment the client chooses the conditions of interaction such as the time and length of the call. Volunteers with little formal qualifications commonly staff these services. Helplines are usually available to clients at extended hours, often 24 hours a day. Typically, no fees are charged to the client.

Telepsychology, on the other hand, has come to mean a service that involves a detailed sharing of information between the mental health practitioner and the client. Telephone counseling refers to any type of psychological service performed over the telephone. Telephone counseling ranges from individual, couple or group psychotherapy with a professional therapist. In telephone counseling, as opposed to Helplines, the counselor aims to provide services over the telephone similarly to the level of service provided in face-to-face consultation at an agreed fee. While these terms and definitions are used, it must be noted that at present the terms used for such services are not strictly adhered to and as such many terms are still used within the area telecommunication based counseling.

Characteristics of Telephone Counseling

The use of the telephone in counseling therapy may include sessions that are entirely conducted via the phone or may be combined with face to face interventions. The longevity of the counseling delivery (that is crisis vs. ongoing) and the type of interaction between the client and counselor, differentiates between the type of counseling provided. Telephone callers may include a variety of individuals. A caller may seek information from a counselor about any issue or topic of interest including advice about a specific issue, general information, referrals, intervention or crises counseling.

Some settings when calling can be less conducive to thoughtful interaction and the discussion of the client's concerns. As such, clients should be encouraged to set aside specific time to optimize counseling interaction. It is not uncommon for clients to call when they have a limited time for conversation. In the context of the variations of calls received and issues dealt with through telephone counseling services, in general, telephone counseling can be divided into four characteristics. These are: intake, triage and assessment, relaying information and follow up.

Intake

Intake is typically the first interaction between the client and the counselor during telephone counseling. It is imperative for the counselor upon intake to ensure they are actually speaking to the intended client and that the phone call is not recorded and not listened to by anyone else. Due to the loss of visual cues, it becomes more critical with telephone counseling to use understandable language and encourage the client to describe in detail the issues of concern. The counselor should listen to understand the client and not interrupt, and should provide the client opportunities to elaborate on the information provided. The counselor can use such techniques as open ended questioning to obtain relevant information.

One challenge that therapists face with this style of counseling is to develop quick trust and rapport. The development of rapport may influence the caller's behavior and attitude towards therapy. Just as physical appearance provides first impression about the therapist in a traditional face to face therapy, so does the voice in telephone counseling. The therapist is encouraged to maintain a steady pace with a soft tone in their voice to demonstrate empathy and understanding. Counseling is best viewed if preceded by empathic discussion and questioning.

Details to be taken and recorded upon intake include specific demographic information about the client, the date and time of the call, the client's name, contact information, the specific questions and concerns of the client and the responses given by the therapist.

Triage and Assessment

Following the collection of general information from the client, the therapist should assess the client's level of knowledge and concern to ascertain the presenting problems and the level of risk. The first primary goal in gathering such information is to determine the client's suitability for telephone counseling, because some clients may not be suitable for counseling through this mode. The following are some examples of when a client may not be suitable for telephone counseling: when there is high risk of harm, when there are high levels of anxiety, when a review of medical records is necessary or when the client presents with severe problems. If committing to telephone counseling with a client, it is important to contract with them a specific scheduled time for the counseling session whereby they do not call at anytime expecting to be able to talk through issues.

Relaying Information

It is also important for the therapist to establish if it is an appropriate time for the client to talk and that the client is in a private location. This is because, unlike face-to-face counseling, the therapist does not have any control over the therapeutic setting in which the client resides for the session. So clarifying the suitability of the place and timing of the session for the client who is calling must occur. It is also very important for the therapist to avoid giving confidential information to a person who is not the client, thus they must refrain from leaving messages on answering machines with identifying information other than name and contact number.

Since there is no face to face interaction between the client and the counselor, verbal and vocal cues are paramount. The therapist must ensure that information is given at a reasonable pace through the use of clear simple terms that avoids jargon and should include pauses to ensure the client understands and allows space for them to respond. The therapist should strive to maintain a compassionate unhurried voice and avoid raising the modulation of words at the end of sentences. The counselor should also be aware of background noises such as computer keyboards and co-workers.

Also, as with any face to face counseling session, continual reassessment of the client's emotional status is important. Because of the difficulty of assessing emotional responses on the telephone, it is particularly important for the counselor to purposefully elicit such responses. Before concluding the call, the therapist must summarize the information briefly and reemphasize any follow up that is necessary.

Follow Up

Documentation should occur immediately following the telephone counseling session. The therapist must document the information provided by the client and other pertinent aspects of the call like with any case notes when seeing clients face to face.

Benefits of Telephone Counseling.

- Save time and money commuting to and from appointments
- It allows you to receive counseling from the comfort of your own home, office or any other place, by using your phone

- It provides you with an added level of anonymity
- You can have therapy sessions while being away from the city
- You can still benefit from therapy even if it is difficult for you to get to a therapist's office

Examples of Nonprofit Telephone Counseling Services

- The Jeevan Aastha Helpline is an initiative by the Gandhi nagar Police Department, Gujarat to provide assistance to those seeking immediate mental health counseling across India. The helpline has a toll free number 1800 233 3330 which can be called on 24/7. The team comprises eight counselors and one senior counselor, all of whom have at least a master's degree in Psychology.
- The Volunteer Emotional Support Helplines (VESH) is an organization representing helplines in 61 countries.
- New Zealand has a community-based, youth-oriented Telephone counseling service, Youthline. Based in 11 local centers around the country, Youthline enlists 1100 volunteers nationwide (100 of whom are working in an online context).
- Australia has a national Telephone counseling service, Lifeline. Also, the larger cities in Australia have other specialized Telephone counseling services, for example: domestic violence, war-victims, youth, gambling, finances, substance abuse, parenting or child care.
- The United States has a government-funded suicide prevention hotline called the National Suicide Prevention Lifeline, which provides 24/7 crisis intervention counseling to suicidal callers. It involves thousands of volunteers at over 120 crisis centers nationwide. It also has a 24/7 National Domestic Violence Hotline.
- In the United Kingdom, well known helplines include ChildLine and The Samaritans. There are a range of specialist helplines for victims of rape, sexual violence and sexual abuse run by third sector organizations, many of which are brought together through membership of The Survivors Trust network.
- In Canada Naseeha is the first Muslim youth helpline.
- Childline India Foundation: CHILDLINE "1098" is a non-profit helpline for children.
- In Egypt, National council for childhood and motherhood provides the only helpline for domestic violence, reproductive health issues, family planning, marriage counseling, health education. Also receive reporting on any form of child trafficking victims. Clients are invited for in-person counseling sessions.

Suicide Prevention

A suicidal person may not ask for help, but that doesn't mean that help isn't wanted. People who take their lives don't want to die—they just want to stop hurting. Suicide prevention starts with recognizing the warning signs and taking them seriously. If you think a friend or family member is considering suicide, you might be afraid to bring up the subject. But talking openly about suicidal thoughts and feelings can save a life.

Common misconceptions about suicide

Myth: People who talk about suicide won't really do it.

Fact: Almost everyone who attempts suicide has given some clue or warning. Don't ignore even indirect references to death or suicide. Statements like "You'll be sorry when I'm gone," "I can't see any way out,"—no matter how casually or jokingly said—may indicate serious suicidal feelings.

Myth: Anyone who tries to kill him/herself must be crazy.

Fact: Most suicidal people are not psychotic or insane. They must be upset, grief-stricken, depressed or despairing, but extreme distress and emotional pain are not necessarily signs of mental illness.

Myth: If a person is determined to kill him/herself, nothing is going to stop them.

Fact: Even the most severely depressed person has mixed feelings about death, wavering until the very last moment between wanting to live and wanting to die. Most suicidal people do not want death; they want the pain to stop. The impulse to end it all, however overpowering, does not last forever.

Myth: People who die by suicide are people who were unwilling to seek help.

Fact: Studies of suicide victims have shown that more than half had sought medical help in the six months prior to their deaths.

Myth: Talking about suicide may give someone the idea.

Fact: You don't give a suicidal person morbid ideas by talking about suicide. The opposite is true—bringing up the subject of suicide and discussing it openly is one of the most helpful things you can do.

Warning Signs of Suicide

Take any suicidal talk or behavior seriously. It's not just a warning sign that the person is thinking about suicide—it's a cry for help.

Most suicidal individuals give warning signs or signals of their intentions. The best way to prevent suicide is to recognize these warning signs and know how to respond if you spot them. If you believe that a friend or family member is suicidal, you can play a role in suicide prevention by pointing out the alternatives, showing that you care, and getting a doctor or psychologist involved.

Major warning signs for suicide include talking about killing or harming oneself, talking or writing a lot about death or dying, and seeking out things that could be used in a suicide attempt, such as weapons and drugs. These signals are even more dangerous if the person has a mood disorder such as depression or bipolar disorder, suffers from alcohol dependence, has previously attempted suicide, or has a family history of suicide.

A more subtle but equally dangerous warning sign of suicide is hopelessness. Studies have found that hopelessness is a strong predictor of suicide. People who feel hopeless may talk about "unbearable" feelings, predict a bleak future, and state that they have nothing to look forward to.

Other warning signs that point to a suicidal mind frame include dramatic mood swings or sudden personality changes, such as going from outgoing to withdrawn or well-behaved to rebellious. A suicidal person may also lose interest in day-to-day activities, neglect his or her appearance, and show big changes in eating or sleeping habits.

Suicide warning signs include:

- Talking about suicide – Any talk about suicide, dying, or self-harm, such as "I wish I hadn't been born," "If I see you again" and "I'd be better off dead."
- Seeking out lethal means – Seeking access to guns, pills, knives, or other objects that could be used in a suicide attempt.
- Preoccupation with death – Unusual focus on death, dying, or violence. Writing poems or stories about death.
- No hope for the future – Feelings of helplessness, hopelessness, and being trapped ("There's no way out"). Belief that things will never get better or change.
- Self-loathing, self-hatred – Feelings of worthlessness, guilt, shame, and self-hatred. Feeling like a burden ("Everyone would be better off without me").
- Getting affairs in order – Making out a will. Giving away prized possessions. Making arrangements for family members.
- Saying goodbye – Unusual or unexpected visits or calls to family and friends. Saying goodbye to people as if they won't be seen again.
- Withdrawing from others – Withdrawing from friends and family. Increasing social isolation. Desire to be left alone.
- Self-destructive behavior – Increased alcohol or drug use, reckless driving, unsafe sex. Taking unnecessary risks as if they have a "death wish."
- Sudden sense of calm – A sudden sense of calm and happiness after being extremely depressed can mean that the person has made a decision to attempt suicide.

Speak up if you're Worried

If you spot the warning signs of suicide in someone you care about, you may wonder if it's a good idea to say anything. What if you're wrong? What if the person gets angry? In such situations, it's natural to feel uncomfortable or afraid. But anyone who talks about suicide or shows other warning signs needs immediate help—the sooner the better.

Talking to a friend or family member about their suicidal thoughts and feelings can be extremely difficult for anyone. But if you're unsure whether someone is suicidal, the best way to find out is to ask. You can't make a person suicidal by showing that you care. In fact, giving a suicidal person the opportunity to express his or her feelings can provide relief from loneliness and pent-up negative feelings, and may prevent a suicide attempt.

Ways to Start a Conversation about Suicide

"I have been feeling concerned about you lately."

"Recently, I have noticed some differences in you and wondered how you are doing."

"I wanted to check in with you because you haven't seemed yourself lately."

Questions you can ask

"When did you begin feeling like this?"

"Did something happen that made you start feeling this way?"

"How can I best support you right now?"

"Have you thought about getting help?"

What you can Say that Helps

"You are not alone in this. I'm here for you."

"You may not believe it now, but the way you're feeling will change."

"I may not be able to understand exactly how you feel, but I care about you and want to help."

"When you want to give up, tell yourself you will hold off for just one more day, hour, minute—whatever you can manage."

DOs and DON'Ts while Talking to a Suicidal Person

Do

- Be yourself. Let the person know you care, that he/she is not alone. The right words are often unimportant. If you are concerned, your voice and manner will show it.
- Listen. Let the suicidal person unload despair, vent anger. No matter how negative the conversation seems, the fact that it exists is a positive sign.
- Be sympathetic, non-judgmental, patient, calm, accepting. Your friend or family member is doing the right thing by talking about his/her feelings.
- Offer hope. Reassure the person that help is available and that the suicidal feelings are temporary. Let the person know that his or her life is important to you.

- Take the person seriously. If the person says things like, "I'm so depressed, I can't go on," ask the question: "Are you having thoughts of suicide?" You are not putting ideas in their head, you are showing that you are concerned, that you take them seriously, and that it's OK for them to share their pain with you.

Don't

- Argue with the suicidal person. Avoid saying things like: "You have so much to live for," "Your suicide will hurt your family," or "Look on the bright side."
- Act shocked, lecture on the value of life, or say that suicide is wrong.
- Promise confidentiality. Refuse to be sworn to secrecy. A life is at stake and you may need to speak to a mental health professional in order to keep the suicidal person safe. If you promise to keep your discussions secret, you may have to break your word.
- Offer ways to fix their problems, or give advice, or make them feel like they have to justify their suicidal feelings. It is not about how bad the problem is, but how badly it's hurting your friend or loved one.
- Blame yourself. You can't "fix" someone's depression. Your loved one's happiness, or lack thereof, is not your responsibility.

Respond Quickly in a Crisis

If a friend or family member tells you that he or she is thinking about death or suicide, it's important to evaluate the immediate danger the person is in. Those at the highest risk for suicide in the near future have a specific suicide PLAN, the MEANS to carry out the plan, a TIME SET for doing it, and an INTENTION to do it.

The following questions can help you assess the immediate risk for suicide:

- Do you have a suicide plan? (PLAN)
- Do you have what you need to carry out your plan (pills, gun, etc.)? (MEANS)
- Do you know when you would do it? (TIME SET)
- Do you intend to take your own life? (INTENTION)

Level of Suicide Risk

Low – Some suicidal thoughts. No suicide plan. Says he or she won't attempt suicide.

Moderate – Suicidal thoughts. Vague plan that isn't very lethal. Says he or she won't attempt suicide.

High – Suicidal thoughts. Specific plan that is highly lethal. Says he or she won't attempt suicide.

Severe – Suicidal thoughts. Specific plan that is highly lethal. Says he or she will attempt suicide.

If a suicide attempt seems imminent, call a local crisis center, dial 911, or take the person to an emergency room. Remove guns, drugs, knives, and other potentially lethal objects from the vicinity but do not, under any circumstances, leave a suicidal person alone.

Offer Help and Support

If a friend or family member is suicidal, the best way to help is by offering an empathetic, listening ear. Let your loved one know that he or she is not alone and that you care. Don't take responsibility, however, for making your loved one well. You can offer support, but you can't get better for a suicidal person. He or she has to make a personal commitment to recovery.

It takes a lot of courage to help someone who is suicidal. Witnessing a loved one dealing with thoughts about ending his or her own life can stir up many difficult emotions. As you're helping a suicidal person, don't forget to take care of yourself. Find someone that you trust—a friend, family member, clergyman, or counselor—to talk to about your feelings and get support of your own.

To Help a Suicidal Person

Get professional help. Do everything in your power to get a suicidal person the help he or she needs. Call a crisis line for advice and referrals. Encourage the person to see a mental health professional, help locate a treatment facility, or take them to a doctor's appointment.

Follow-up on treatment. If the doctor prescribes medication, make sure your friend or loved one takes it as directed. Be aware of possible side effects and be sure to notify the physician if the person seems to be getting worse. It often takes time and persistence to find the medication or therapy that's right for a particular person.

Be proactive. Those contemplating suicide often don't believe they can be helped, so you may have to be more proactive at offering assistance. Saying, "Call me if you need anything" is too vague. Don't wait for the person to call you or even to return your calls. Drop by, call again, and invite the person out.

Encourage positive lifestyle changes, such as a healthy diet, plenty of sleep, and getting out in the sun or into nature for at least 30 minutes each day. Exercise is also extremely important as it releases endorphins, relieves stress, and promotes emotional well-being.

Make a safety plan. Help the person develop a set of steps he or she promises to follow during a suicidal crisis. It should identify any triggers that may lead to a suicidal crisis, such as an anniversary of a loss, alcohol, or stress from relationships. Also include contact numbers for the person's doctor or therapist, as well as friends and family members who will help in an emergency.

Remove potential means of suicide, such as pills, knives, razors, or firearms. If the person is likely to take an overdose, keep medications locked away or give out only as the person needs them.

Continue your support over the long haul. Even after the immediate suicidal crisis has passed, stay in touch with the person, periodically checking in or dropping by. Your support is vital to ensure your friend or loved one remains on the recovery track.

Postvention

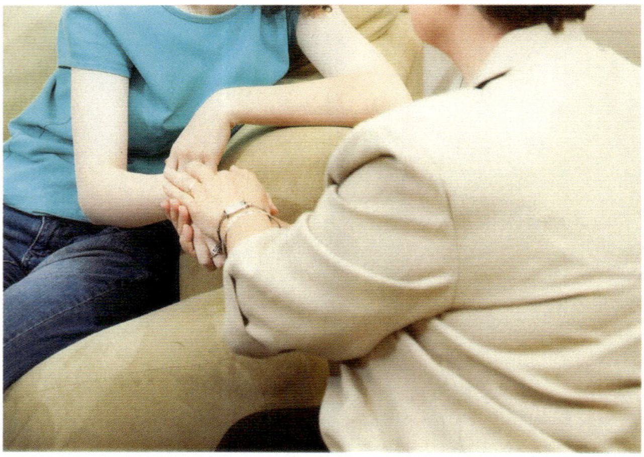

Postvention refers to a range of activities following a suicide. Suicide postvention is part of the overall spectrum of suicide prevention activities. Although postvention occurs after a death by suicide, it is preventive in that it reduces suicide risk by identifying and supporting the emotional and mental health needs of the survivors. Youth are more susceptible to suicide contagion than older age groups. Postvention includes procedures to alleviate the distress of suicidally bereaved individuals, reduce the risk of imitative suicidal behavior, and promote the healthy recovery of the affected community. Postvention can also take many forms depending on the situation in which the suicide takes place. Schools and colleges may include postvention strategies in overall crisis plans. These strategies are designed to prevent suicide clusters and to help students cope with the emotions of loss that follow the suicide of a friend. Individual and group counseling may be offered for survivors (people affected by the suicide of an individual).

The Suicide Aftercare Association, a public charity, was formed to reduce the possibility of suicide contagion and secondary suicides by performing bio-hazardous cleaning of suicide attempt and completion scenes so families are relieved of this burden.

Crisis Response Programs

Responding to Loss (RTL)

Responding to Loss (RTL) is one of the crisis response programs that have been used to deal with postvention at high schools. This program is part of the Community Action for Youth Survival (CAYS), which is a three-year adolescent suicide prevention project serving three counties in the Chicago area. The objective of RTL is to provide strategies that will help high school crisis teams develop a structured response to the suicide of any student or member of the staff. There are three components to this program. The first is Preparing for Crisis Training, the second is Peer Witness Intervention, and the third is Crisis Consultation. This program proved to be quite successful during its trial and the participants of the program were generally satisfied with the training that they received. As a result of this program, several schools have developed or revised their crisis team in response to a suicide. They have done this by following the Preparing for Crisis training aspect of the program and also through consulting with the CAYS program.

Loss

The LOSS Program includes a first-response team with the objectives of delivering immediate services to the survivors of a suicide at the time of the death. This team is made up of para-professional survivor volunteers and staff members of the Baton Rouge Crisis Intervention Center, located in Baton Rouge, Louisiana. The LOSS Program is different from other postvention programs in several ways. First, the LOSS team physically goes to the scenes of the suicides to begin helping the survivors to cope with their loss as close to the event of death as possible. Members of this team can provide access to the needed resources and can begin the grieving process at the scene of the death. Second, since the LOSS team includes survivor volunteers at the scene, an immediate and meaningful bond is established between the newly bereaved individuals and the para-professional surveyor team members. This bond allows for the start of a conversation about the grief and the potential for hope of a suicide between the bereaved and the crisis team members. Third, the LOSS team has a strong relationship with other first responders, such as law enforcement, emergency services, fire departments, funeral home representatives, and more. This relationship allows the newly bereaved to have a larger variety of choices in regards to coping with a suicide compared to other survivors who might not have access to this program. This model of postvention provides referrals for additional support to all survivors and individuals at the scene of the suicide The model of the LOSS Program has changed the scene of the suicide to a more “concerned and caring environment” for all individuals and survivors.

Senior Peer Counseling

Senior peer counseling, a.k.a. Peer counseling for seniors, provides senior citizens with a trained volunteer counselor to provide assistance with emotional support and encouragement to those who are experiencing life changes that often accompany aging. Seniors typically use counseling to discover ways to deal with grief, loss, physical limitations, financial issues, mild depression, family relationships, loneliness, isolation, housing situations, anxiety, change in cognitive function, and care giving for a spouse.

The original idea of Senior Peer Counseling was developed in 1977 by Evelyn Freeman, Ph.D. (1917–2013). She first created a program called Senior Health and Peer Counseling of Santa Monica, California. In 1986 in collaboration with others, she produced "Peer Counseling for Seniors: A Trainer's Guide". As a result, various groups utilized her trainer's guide and Senior Peer Counseling programs became available in many California counties as well as in South Carolina, Colorado, Oregon, New Mexico, and Washington. The program is also available in Europe, Canada, and Japan. Sponsorship of the program in those locations comes from county health services, interfaith councils, senior citizen advocacy groups, and non-profit organizations. These Senior Peer Counseling programs vary widely in their methods, and no one program is alike. However, they all operate in the spirit of Evelyn Freeman's vision of Senior Peer Counseling. In addition, even though no two programs are exactly alike, there is an organization called the American Association of Senior Peer Counseling that tries to bring together all of the various Senior Peer Counseling agencies to share opportunities for networking and information.

Program Design Characteristics

In general, Senior Peer Counseling volunteers are trained to provide one-on-one, (counselor and client) confidential counseling to other persons 50 years of age or older. The counseling sessions are goal-oriented or supportive and are in general one hour per week. The sessions are held in the client's home, a senior citizen center, or another confidential setting and are closely supervised by professionals, i.e., psychologists, marriage and family therapists, or social workers, who intervene, as appropriate, with suggestions about how to handle situations with clients or to provide resources. Confidentiality is only broken in exceptional circumstances, such as when there is suspected child or elder abuse or when the client reports he or she is at risk of suicide, homicide, or grave disability. In these events, counseling's have specific reporting instructions to assure the safety of everyone concerned. Referrals to Senior Peer Counseling programs are often made by Adult Protective Services agencies, home health workers, hospitals, social workers, registered nurses, senior housing, or other agencies serving senior citizens. Elders may become aware of the program through postings in senior citizen centers, senior housing, or other agencies serving senior citizens, and may self-refer into the program.

Effectiveness

Seniors counseling can be effective because the counselors often have had life experiences similar to their clients. In contrast, professional counselors may unintentionally create a power imbalance with older clients unfamiliar with formal counseling and many senior clients will not seek formal counseling due to cost or perceived stigma. Senior peer counseling programs, therefore, may provide a more comfortable and supportive environment for the client.

In 2010-2011, a study of 43 senior peer counseling clients in San Mateo County, California, was conducted. The study concluded that the clients had discussed personal issues in their lives more often with their senior peer counselors than with anyone else including family, friends, and neighbors. The study also found that 75% of the clients had reported the senior peer counseling had "helped a lot", especially with their concerns about food, health, loneliness, and sadness. Twenty-three percent reported it had "helped a little bit" and 3% reported it "had not helped at all".

Active Listening

Active listening is an essential skill counselors can exploit to develop a positive and healthy interaction with a client.

Active listening intentionally focuses on who you are listening to, whether in a group or one-on-one, in order to understand what he or she is saying. As the listener, you should then be able to repeat back in your own words what they have said to their satisfaction. This does not mean you agree with, but rather understand, what they are saying.

There are numerous situations in which counselors can utilize active listening to build rapport with clients and improve overall communication. Some of these are explored below.

Information: Getting a Clear Picture

This means asking questions to find out about needs, instructions and context of a client. Counselors should check back to ensure they've heard and understood the relevant details, and that the client agrees on the facts.

- Aim of the speaker: To tell them what you want.
- Aim of the listener: To find out and confirm what they are saying.

Affirmation: Affirming, Acknowledging, Exploring the Problem

Listening actively to a person who would benefit from having their problem acknowledged by the counselor.

The problem may or may not involve the counselor directly. Counselors may reflect back the client's feelings and perhaps the content of the problem with a single statement of acknowledgment or during a dialogue over a period of time, exploring the difficulty in more depth.

- Aim of the speaker: To tell someone (counselor) about the problem.
- Aim of the listener: To help them hear what they are saying. The listener is assisting the speaker to explore the problem further, so the speaker can find greater clarity and understanding for themselves.

Inflammation: Responding to a Complaint

When clients tell the counselor they are unhappy with them, criticizing them, complaining about them, or getting it off their chest, the best thing the counselor can do (although challenging) is to effectively listen.

- Aim of the speaker: To tell the counselor that they are the problem.
- Aim of the listener: Let them know that they have taken in what they are saying and to defuse the strong emotion.

When there is conflict it is very common to blame the other person. It is challenging to be objective when the emotional level is high. Active listening is an effective tool to reduce the emotion of a situation. Every time the counselor correctly labels an emotion, the intensity of it dissipates like bursting a bubble.

The speaker feels heard and understood. Once the emotional level has been reduced, reasoning abilities can function more effectively. If the emotions are high, counselors should deal with the emotions first by using active listening skills. Effective use of active listening skills can turn a challenging situation into a co-operative situation.

Below is a list of what a counselor should and shouldn't do in relation to applying active listening skills to a therapeutic situation.

Things a Counselor Should do

1. Give the person speaking their full attention.
2. Repeat the conversation back to them, in their own words, providing their interpretation or understanding of the client's meaning (paraphrasing).
3. By reflecting the content of what is being said back to the speaker, check their understanding of the message.
4. Be as accurate in summarizing the client's meaning as much as they can.
5. Try again if their paraphrasing is not accurate or well received.
6. Feed back to the client their feelings as well as the content (e.g. how did you feel when? How did that affect you? It looks like that made you really angry).
7. Challenge in a non-threatening and subtle manner.
    - Statement: "This is hopeless." Paraphrasing: "It seems hopeless to you right now".
    - Statement: "There is nothing I can do". Paraphrasing: "You can't find anything that would fix it".
8. Not try to force conversation, allow silences — and be aware of body language, notice changes and respond accordingly.

Things a Counselor Should not do

1. Talking about themselves and introducing their own reactions or well intended comments.
2. Changing topics and thinking about what they will say next.

3. Advising, diagnosing, reassuring, encouraging, criticizing or baiting a client.
4. Using "mm" or "ah ah" exclusively or inappropriately or parrot their words.
5. Pretending to have understood the person or their meaning if they haven't.
6. Allowing the client to drift to a less significant topic, because they feel the counselor doesn't understand.
7. Fixing, changing or improving what they have said — or finishing their sentences for them.
8. Filling every space with talk.
9. Ignoring their feelings in the situation.

Uses of Active Listening

Active listening is used in a wide variety of situations, including public interest advocacy, community organizing, tutoring, medical workers talking to patients, HIV counseling, helping suicidal persons, management, counseling and journalistic settings. In groups it may aid in reaching consensus. It may also be used in casual conversation or small talk to build understanding, though this can be interpreted as condescending.

A listener can use several degrees of active listening, each resulting in a different quality of communication.

The proper use of active listening results in getting people to open up, avoiding misunderstandings, resolving conflict, and building trust. In a medical context, benefits may include increased patient satisfaction, improved cross-cultural communication, improved outcomes, or decreased litigation.

Active listening can be lifted by the active listening observation scale.

Counting Method

The Counting Method is a clinical technique for the treatment of the symptoms of Post-traumatic Stress Disorder (PTSD), originated by Frank Ochberg. Specifically, the procedure aims to desensitize clients to intrusive traumatic memories. Because traumatic memories are vivid and frightening, and arise unexpectedly, they can cause significant secondary effects on the sufferer, including diminished self-confidence, decreased sense of security, and compromised beliefs about one's own sanity. With the goals of ameliorating the anxiety accompanying traumatic memories and enhancing the sense of mastery over intrusive recollections, the Counting Method can contribute to the overall therapeutic endeavor with PTSD clients

Procedure

Phase One: Preparation

Presenting the Rationale: The therapist begins by reviewing the rationale for the method with the client. The therapist emphasizes the role of avoidance in maintaining the arousal to the stimulus, and the need to remember the trauma from beginning to end. The established effectiveness of exposure therapies is explained. The therapist underscores how the counting procedure will help by having a definite end, and by allowing for private recall. Generally the counting procedure is introduced early in the session to allow sufficient time for adequately processing the memory. Most procedures require about a half hour to complete.

Identification of the Index Trauma: The procedure is applied to one, specific memory at a time; thus this memory must be identified prior to the procedure. The therapist will ask the client to describe the outlines of the trauma briefly, without details that might arouse too much affect prior to the procedure. Next, the therapist helps the client identify a specific time-point just prior to the traumatic event, and also an end point--a time in which the client was no longer in acute danger. Too narrowly defining the time period will leave the client too aroused at the end of the counting, while too broadly defining it (e.g., over days) does not allow the client sufficient time to engage with the worst part of the memory. The middle or most traumatic part of the memory is not anchored because this is likely to arouse affect and unnaturally define an often chaotically-experienced moment. It is often surprising what becomes identified as the most arousing part of the memory.

Initial Instruction: Once the memory is anchored, the therapist indicates that they are ready to begin, and says, "What we are about to do is to go back and remember this event. I will be with you, counting slowly from 1 to 100. Together we will re-visit the scene and then return. OK?" The therapist then pauses while looking at the client. This both emphasizes the collaborative nature of the endeavor, and demarcates a boundary between the normal interaction of client and therapist, and the special interaction to be experienced during the counting procedure. The instructions, which are delivered in a somewhat formal tone, follow:

Complete Instructions: "I am going to count from 1 to 100, at a rate of about one number per second. I would like you to recall the memory from the beginning, at about the point that you, letting the worst part of the memory crest as the counting goes into the 40s through the 60s. Try to reach the end of the memory, the point at which you, as the counting approaches the 80s. Midway through the 90s, I will say "back here" to let you know that we are near the end, and that you should be coming out of the past and returning to the present. I ask you not to talk during the counting. It is usually best if you close your eyes or look away from me. OK, I'd like you to sit in a comfortable, resting position. Are you comfortable? Then let us begin."

Phase Two: Counting Procedure

The therapist uses a calm and friendly voice and counts out loud from 1 to 100, maintaining a steady rhythm of about one number per second. Be sure to avoid the common uplift in tone when one reaches the 8 and 9 of a series: 27, 28, 29, 30. Learning how to breathe and count at the same time is important. The therapist speaks "to" instead of "at" the client, and looks at the client so as to monitor bodily reactions. The therapist remains quiet, that is, does not shift position, handle papers, or looks away. It is important to notice if the client is becoming aroused, that is, showing tears, making grimaces, shuddering, clenching hands, or breathing more deeply or quickly. In contrast, there may be no sign of distress, which may mean that the client was unable to recall the traumatic memory, or that the method did not elicit a great deal of affect.

Normally, the memories evoked during counting will be no more intense than spontaneous remembering. If the client becomes overwhelmed during the counting and is in tears, the therapist continues, since catharsis is common. In the unusual circumstance where the client stops the procedure and opens his or her eyes, the therapist needs to assess whether something is distracting the client (e.g., the counting is too loud), or whether the person needs more preparation before attempting the procedure. Similarly, the therapist may become slightly aroused by imagining what the client is experiencing, which may impact on the rhythm and steadiness of their counting.

On 94, the therapist says, "back here" to help remind clients to bring themselves from the memory back to the present. This is especially helpful for those clients who have had a deeply engaging experience, or who have become partially dissociated.

Phase Three: The Moment After the Counting

The moment after the counting is given greater emphasis in the revised method. Clients often look dazed or thoughtful after the counting and may not speak for some time. They may feel some sense of accomplishment, relief, or some residual terror from the original event. They may have remembered aspects of the event that were forgotten or repressed. They may be embarrassed or unwilling to discuss what happened. The therapist should respect this moment of silence and stay silent until addressed by the client. Some clients may remain so deep in thought that they do not speak for several minutes. The therapist should never address the client, make evaluative or analytical comments, or indicate an expectation of a response from the client during this moment.

This moment parallels the homecoming experience of traumatized clients, when they first face other people to report their trauma. Many clients will be filled with feelings of humiliation or shame over what happened to them. They cannot believe they are worthy as people, having been "soiled" by the experience. By looking directly at clients and nonverbally conveying warmth and support, the therapist acknowledges their pain, as well as communicates admiration for their courage to do this work. The therapist's calm patience during this moment also demonstrates his/her tolerance for the traumatic material: an absence of the need to contain his/her anxiety with a burst of helpful advice or reassurance. Once the client speaks to the therapist, the therapist may then respond with an affirmation: "That was something. You made it there and back again." Instead of a shaming or rejecting "welcome back," the therapist specifically puts words to the look and smile, affirming the courage of the client to revisit the trauma. In training sessions, this capacity to tolerate the moment of silence has been the most challenging feature of the Counting Method for many therapists.

Phase Four: Formal Review

The therapist then asks the client, *"Now, can you describe what you just remembered during the counting?"* It is important to note that a description of the event per se is not requested, only what was remembered during the procedure. Usually a detailed narrative from the client follows. The therapist takes notes in order to allow uninterrupted reporting by the client and a more accurate accounting. It allows time between the solitary act of private recall and the collaborative endeavor of redefining a piece of personal history. Many clients appreciate their therapist taking notes, since eye contact is less important than careful attention to the details of the story.

Sometimes the client has difficulty remembering or is still dazed by the intensity of recall. The person's narrative may be fragmented, or described in a vague and general manner. The therapist can aid the recall if necessary by asking, *"What did you recall in the 20s and 30s?"*

After the client has concluded, the therapist reads back from the notes in as close to a word-by-word repetition as is possible, except *in the second person* (e.g., "you went up the stairs to look into the bedroom."). The purpose is to communicate understanding of the client's experience in its totality, and to allow the client to hear the trauma again, but now from a more distanced perspective as a listener. We have found that clients are extremely sensitive to even minor paraphrasing or interpretive insertions that do not exactly match their experience. If they indicate verbally or nonverbally that you have made an error, correct yourself and repeat the sentence correctly, noting the change in your notes. As in client-centered therapy, the intent is to communicate that the client has been accurately heard and to avoid evaluative comments about the client's behavior during the traumatic event. We have found this to be especially difficult for many clinicians learning this technique. Apparently there is a tremendous pressure experienced by therapists to insert themselves into the trauma narrative, most likely out of a desire to help the client, but also possibly out of discomfort with taking in the traumatic material.

After reading back the story, the therapist affirms the client's experience, *"You went through a terrible experience. Yet you survived it, and are able to remember it when you wish."* By concluding the review of the trauma with an affirmation, the important message-- you are a survivor, and you have the ability to gain control over your traumatic memories--is reinforced. Often the client will have difficulty accepting such support due to the shame or embarrassment occasioned by remembering the trauma.

Phase Five: Reflection and Closure

The final step is reflection and closure. The purpose of this step is to help clients distance themselves from the memory and diminish strong affect. The therapist asks the client about the procedure itself, rather than the traumatic memory, and draws the client's attention onto the present. Questions concerning whether the counting was too loud or distracting, whether 100 was long enough, are asked. It is very common for clients during their first counting session to have difficulty simultaneously listening to the counting and engaging in their memory. Later, most have been able to integrate the two channels, weaving the counting into their remembering. Clients that initially do not hear the counting are often deeply immersed in the trauma; while clients that cannot engage with the memory because of the counting are relying on more avoidant defenses. Many clients report periods of both experiences during the counting. The content of the client's perceptions is not as important as having them distance themselves intellectually from the experience.

At the end of the session, the therapist gives another affirmation, such as *"You did well. You remembered. You turned the tape on and you turned the tape off."* The purpose of this affirmation is to end the session on a positive note, with the client composed enough to leave the office and secure enough to continue therapy. This comment also underscores the sense of mastery embedded within the technique.

Optionally, you may also instruct them: *"In the future, when you recall that event, you can remember how we revisited the scene together, how you heard me counting, and how you turned off the tape when I said 94."* Some clients have reported that this instruction has been helpful to them. Others have even counted to themselves while remembering the event.

If there is still time in the session, the therapist can shift directly onto other topics. It is generally not recommended to continue to work on the index trauma using other techniques during this session.

Use of SUDS: Many therapists will incorporate the use of Subjective Units of Distress into this method, by asking the client at the very beginning and at the end of the Counting session to rate the degree to which the specific memory distresses them, on a scale from 0 (not at all) to 10 (the worst it has ever been). As in other methods, generally one works with the same memory until the SUDS drop to 2 or less.

Length of Treatment

When the traumatic memory is circumscribed and uncomplicated, three to five counting sessions are usually sufficient to help the client feel a sense of mastery and control over the intrusive recollections of that particular trauma. Some traumatic memories, however, are multidimensional and complex, with many meanings for the client, and may require a number of consecutive sessions or several sessions spaced months apart. Anchor points may be shifted to "zoom in" on more specific sections of a memory, or extended to take in important aspects not previously included. Even when relief is experienced, some clients may request additional sessions to confront other issues related to the trauma or to specifically work on modifying their memories. Some clients have benefited in later stages of treatment by adding creative modifications to their memory during the counting, such as changing the ending so they escape the injury, are rescued, or are able to punish their assailants. These interventions appear to increase the client's cognitive flexibility, thereby aiding the further integration of the memory into the client's normative schemas. The result is a further reduction in the client's fear.

Management of Challenging Situations

1. Client becomes very emotionally aroused while describing memory in the Preparation Phase. You may have asked the client to describe too many details of the memory. Attempt to calm the client through reassurance and direct them to describe only the trauma in general. Point out that alleviating the pressure they are feeling through a desensitization procedure will be a welcome relief.

2. Client asks you why you think this will work. Tell them you can never be certain, but that clinical and research experience gives you a great deal of confidence in the method, and then review the rationale presented earlier in this manual.

3. Client stops the procedure during the counting. In this unlikely event, you will need to inquire why they could not continue with it, point out how that indicates there is a need for desensitization, and then review the rationale for the procedure again. Obviously if they continue to refuse the procedure, you will have to delay it.

4. In the Reflection Phase, the client says that the counting out loud was distracting. You should note their comment, but this is a very common form of avoidance which almost always recedes in repeated counting sessions.

5. Client becomes overwhelmed during the counting and is in tears. Generally, you should continue the counting, since catharsis is common. You may say, "I'm with you," or "You're doing fine," one or two times to provide additional support.

6. The client appears too aroused or too "deep in thought" at the end of the

counting. Wait silently and allow the client room to process the experience in their own way.

7. Client is not able to describe what s/he had just remembered, and instead, discusses the memory in a general or vague way. Help the client be more specific by asking for more details, and by inquiring "by the numbers": "what were you remembering around 40?"

8. Client is reluctant to disclose what s/he had just remembered. Give the client time to digest what happened, and then gently encourage them to tell you what they experienced, possibly also inquiring by the numbers. If the client insists, then you can acknowledge their wish, and proceed to the affirmations.

9. Client asks you for your opinion about their trauma after you read back the trauma narrative. Repeat the affirmation that they went through a (e.g., terrible, awful, horrendous, devastating) experience, and that it takes a lot of courage to review these memories. Never make an evaluative comment about how they behaved during the traumatic event.

10. Client is unable to accept the therapists' affirmations. Either you did not deliver the affirmations in an empathic manner, or more likely the client has difficulty accepting your support due to the shame or embarrassment occasioned by remembering the trauma. This is not uncommon early in the counting procedure. In either case, you should continue with the procedure as indicated.

Havening

The havening techniques are a healing modality that is designed to help individuals overcome problems that are the consequence of traumatic encoding. The havening techniques belong to a larger group of methods called psych sensory therapies, which use sensory input to alter thought, mood and behavior. The havening techniques are a system comprised of protocols and methods that uses touch as a therapeutic tool which we call Havening Touch®. The havening techniques have three distinct applications, one is for emotional disturbances and encoded psychological trauma, second is for wellness, stress management, and peak performance, and the third is as a self-help tool. Therefore, the havening techniques can be used within a psycho-therapeutic setting with professional mental health care clinicians that have been fully trained and certified in the havening techniques. In addition, The havening techniques can be used by non-licensed practitioners as a protocol for coaching sessions, or as a tool in allied health care practice by individuals that have been fully trained and certified in the havening techniques. The havening techniques can also be used as a self-help technique and shared with family members and friends.

Problems that Havening Techniques Address

The consequences of traumatic encoding and stressful life events can be physical and psychological. While we can't provide any guarantees, the havening techniques have been shown to help with Phobias, Chronic pain, Distressing memories (broken relationships, shocking news, loss, embarrassment, etc.), Victims of natural disasters (hurricanes, floods, etc.), and man-made (war, fire, assault, home intrusion, etc.) events, Anger, Fear of Abandonment, Grief cravings, PTSD, Panic attacks, Emotional eating and many other problems.

Are the Havening Techniques a Distraction or not

The havening techniques are not a distraction, but distraction does plays a role in them. Each distraction component has a biological correlate. This means there is a purpose to each action. Our experience is that most clients do not believe it will work and are astonished when it does. The strangeness of the method and its effects on their mind makes them ask the following questions.

Permanency of Results of a Session of the Havening Techniques

While the havening techniques is a relatively new healing approach and has yet to be fully researched, we've observed that after successfully applying the havening techniques it appears to be permanent in most cases. This is because the havening techniques are designed to alter the biological structure of the brain. The occasional return of symptoms implies either the traumatic core has not yet been found or the problem has been encoded in a different way. In particular, addictive and obsessive/compulsive behaviors, certain pain syndromes and vasovagal (e.g. fainting) issues often need reinforcement or cannot be treated at the present time. No healing method or therapy works for all problems.

Is the Havening Technique a Form of Hypnosis

No. The havening techniques do not involve a hypnotic trance. The client is always aware of their feelings, thoughts, and surroundings and participates fully in the process.

Workings of the Havening Technique

We believe the consequences of trauma and stressful life events are stored in the brain and are activated by conscious or inadvertent recall. Once this recall occurs, symptoms are generated. This activation also makes the pathway that generates these feelings subject to disruption. The havening techniques are designed to disrupt this pathway through a process called synaptic depotentiation; literally, it is as if we darken a room by pulling a plug on a lit lamp. Although we can't provide any guarantees, after performing The havening techniques the emotions and sometimes even the ability to recall the memory can be extinguished.

References

- In the Company of Others: An Introduction to Communication. New York: Oxford University Press. 2010. pp. 157–66. ISBN 0-19-533630-5. OCLC 276930486
- What-is-online-therapy-2795752: verywellmind.com, Retrieved 19 May 2018
- Lang F, Floyd MR, Beine KL (2000). "Clues to patients' explanations and concerns about their illnesses. A call for active listening". Arch Fam Med. 9 (3): 222–27. doi:10.1001/archfami.9.3.222. PMID 10728107
- Introduction-to-telephone-counselling: aipc.net.au, Retrieved 10 June 2018
- "The Counseling Center- Hotlines - Caldwell University, New Jersey". Caldwell University, New Jersey. Retrieved 2016-03-01
- Gregory E. Simon et al, "Telephone Psychotherapy and Telephone Care Management for Primary Care Patients Starting Antidepressant Treatment", Journal of American Medical Association, August 25, 2004, Vol 292, No. 8
- Suicide-postvention-prevention: heretohelp.bc.ca, Retrieved 20 April 2018
- Reese, R., Conoley, C., Brossart, D. (2006) The Attractiveness of Telephone Counseling: An Empirical Investigation of Client Perceptions. Journal of Counseling & Development. 84:1, 54-60
- "An Evaluation of Crisis Hotline Outcomes – Part 2: Suicidal Callers". Atypon-link.com. January 1, 1970. Retrieved November 20, 2011
- Principles-of-active-listening: counsellingconnection.com, Retrieved 28 March 2018
- Worthington, Debra (2016). Listening: Processes, Functions and Competency. New York: Routledge. p. 87. ISBN 9780132288545
- Vangelisti, A.; Knapp, M.; Daly, J. (1990). "Conversational narcissism". Communication Monographs. 57: 251–74. doi:10.1080/03637759009376202

5

Psychotherapy

Psychotherapy is the practice of using psychological methods for changing a person's behavior and helping him/her overcome problems so as to improve his/her mental health and well-being. This chapter has been carefully written to provide an easy understanding of the different therapies under the scope of psychotherapy, such as art, dance, narrative, music, emotional and family therapy, among others.

Psychotherapy, or talk therapy, is a way to help people with a broad variety of mental illnesses and emotional difficulties. Psychotherapy can help eliminate or control troubling symptoms so a person can function better and can increase well-being and healing.

Problems helped by psychotherapy include difficulties in coping with daily life; the impact of trauma, medical illness or loss, like the death of a loved one; and specific mental disorders, like depression or anxiety. There are several different types of psychotherapy and some types may work better with certain problems or issues. Psychotherapy may be used in combination with medication or other therapies.

Therapy Sessions

Therapy may be conducted in an individual, family, couple, or group setting, and can help both children and adults. Most sessions are 30 to 50 minutes long. Both patient and therapist need to be actively involved in psychotherapy. The trust and relationship between a person and his/her therapist is essential to working together effectively and benefiting from psychotherapy.

Psychotherapy can be short-term (a few sessions), dealing with immediate issues, or long-term (months or years), dealing with longstanding and complex issues. The goals of treatment and arrangements for how often and how long to meet are planned jointly by the patient and therapist.

Confidentiality is a basic requirement of psychotherapy. Also, although patients share personal feelings and thoughts, intimate physical contact with a therapist is never appropriate, acceptable, or useful.

Psychotherapy is sometimes called "the talking cure."

Psychotherapy is sometimes called a "talking treatment" because it uses talking, rather than medication.

Some forms of psychotherapy last only a few sessions, while others are long-term, lasting for months or years. Sessions are usually for 1 hour, once a week, and they follow a carefully structured process.

Sessions may be one-to-one, in pairs, or in groups. Techniques can include other forms of communication, such as drama, narrative story, or music. A psychotherapist may be a psychologist, a marriage and family therapist, a licensed clinical social worker or mental health counselor, a psychiatric nurse practitioner, psychoanalyst, or psychiatrist.

Psychotherapy can be used to help a range of people. The following feelings are signs that an individual might benefit from this type of therapy:

- Overwhelming feelings of sadness or helplessness.
- An inability to cope with everyday problems.
- Difficulty concentrating on work or studies most of the time.
- Drinking too much, taking drugs, or being aggressive to an extent that is harming themselves or others.

- A sense that problems never improve, despite receiving help from friends and family.
- Feeling constantly on edge or worrying unnecessarily.

Types of Psychotherapy

Behavioral Therapy

Behavioral therapy helps clients to understand how changes in behavior can lead to changes in how they feel. It focuses on increasing the person's engagement in positive or socially reinforcing activities. The approach assesses what the client is doing, and then tries to increase the chance of having positive experiences. The goal is for desirable behavior responses to replace undesirable ones. Behavioral therapy can help people whose emotional distress stems from behaviors that they engage in.

Cognitive Therapy

Cognitive therapy starts with the idea that what we think shapes how we feel. Depression, for example, may stem from having thoughts or beliefs that are not based on evidence, such as "I am useless," or "Everything goes wrong because of me." Changing these beliefs can change a person's view of events, and their emotional state. Cognitive therapy looks at current thinking and communication patterns, rather than the past. The therapist works with the client to confront and challenge inappropriate thoughts by encouraging different ways of viewing a situation. Cognitive therapy can help in treating conditions such as post-traumatic stress disorder (PTSD). Cognitive behavioral therapy (CBT) pairs cognitive with behavioral therapy, to address both thoughts and behaviors.

Interpersonal Therapy

Psychotherapy can involve movement, drama and music, can help people of any age, and can be done in groups, pairs, or one-on-one.

This approach focuses on interpersonal relationships. Depression, for instance, may stem from a person's relationship with others. Learning skills for improving communication patterns may help the client to manage the depression. First, the therapist may help the client to identify relevant emotions, and where these are coming from. Then they can help them to express the emotions in a healthier way. For example, someone who responds to feeling neglected by getting angry may trigger a negative reaction in a loved one. Learning to express the hurt and anxiety calmly can increase the chances of the other person reacting positively. The client learns to modify their approach to interpersonal problems, understand them, and manage them more constructively. People who might benefit from this type of therapy include individuals who are eager to please others at their own expense, or who find that they have volatile interpersonal relationships.

Family Therapy

A family therapist looks at symptoms in the family context. Some conditions require the treatment of the family unit. An example is when a client has depression because of marital problems. Cognitive therapy, behavioral therapy, and especially interpersonal therapy may help. Identifying family patterns that contribute to behavior disorder or mental illness can help family members to break negative habits and patterns. Often, family therapy focuses on improving communication within the family. Participants learn new ways of listening and how to ask and respond to questions openly rather than defensively. Family therapy generally involves discussion and problem-solving sessions with the client and the family, as a group, in couples, or one-to-one.

Group Therapy

A group therapy session usually involves 6-12 clients and one therapist. The participants have similar problems, and they benefit from the therapist, and by observing how others handle their issues and respond to feedback. Getting feedback from other people with related problems can give a new perspective and help to facilitate improvement and change. Group therapy can help those who may feel a sense of isolation because of their issue. Although participating in a group may seem intimidating, it helps people to realize that they are not alone, and that others share the same problem. The sense of support is generally powerful and many participants in group therapy find the experience rewarding.

Psychodynamic Therapy

Psychodynamic therapy, or insight-oriented therapy, focuses on the deep-seated causes of behavior. For instance, patterns of behavior stemming from a person's upbringing or earlier life experiences, which continue to impact present-day behaviors. The aim is to increase self-awareness and understanding of how the past affects present behavior. The client will consider unresolved issues and symptoms that stem from past dysfunctional relationships. Unresolved problems can underlie behaviors such as drug or alcohol abuse. This can help people to understand the source of their emotional distress, usually by exploring motives, needs, and defenses that they are not aware of. Psychodynamic therapy can help people whose symptoms have not been resolved by other forms of psychotherapy.

Art Therapy

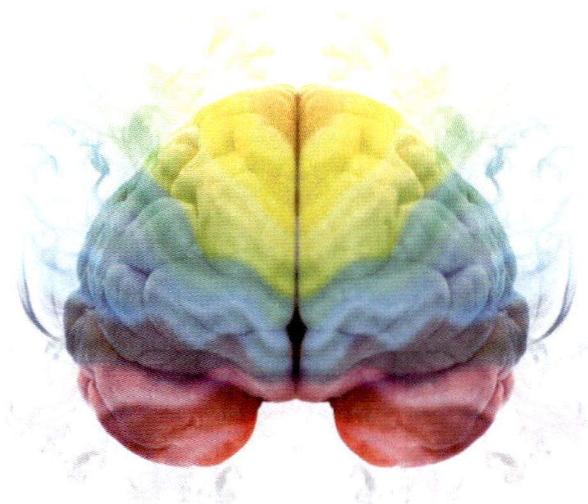

Art therapy is a form of psychotherapy that uses art media as its primary mode of expression and communication. Within this context, art is not used as diagnostic tool but as a medium to address emotional issues which may be confusing and distressing.

Art therapists work with children, young people, adults and the elderly. Clients may have a wide range of difficulties, disabilities or diagnoses. These include emotional, behavioral or mental health problems, learning or physical disabilities, life-limiting conditions, neurological conditions and physical illnesses.

Art therapy is provided in groups or individually, depending on clients' needs. It is not a recreational activity or an art lesson, although the sessions can be enjoyable. Clients do not need to have any previous experience or expertise in art.

Although influenced by psychoanalysis, art therapists have been inspired by theories such as attachment-based psychotherapy and have developed a broad range of client-centered approaches such as psycho-educational, mindfulness and metallization-based treatments, compassion-focused and cognitive analytic therapies, and socially engaged practice.

Different Art Mediums

The beauty of art therapy is its versatility. While of course there is the option to work with paint and canvas, there are many other mediums to choose from. Take a look at the list below for examples:

Painting

Putting paint to paper is one of the purest forms of art and allows you an immense amount of freedom. Being faced with a blank canvas may be intimidating at first, but your art therapist should guide you by giving you prompts and exercises. With painting you can use bright, vivid colors or muted, darker colors to help represent what you are trying to convey. Don't worry if you have never painted before, your therapist will be able to teach you basic techniques so you are able to explore the medium to its fullest.

Crayons/Chalk

Allowing you to blend and create unique effects, many people like to use crayons and chalk within art therapy. Crayons may also instill happy memories as they often represent experiences from your childhood. If you have an effect in mind, don't hesitate to ask your therapist for guidance so they can tell you the best way to achieve it.

Sculpting

Usually this is done with clay or some other pliable material. Sculpting 3D models can help bring your emotions to life. You can also work with duller colors if you find bright hues too stimulating. Much of sculpting involves trial and error, so feel free to experiment with different concepts and materials.

Drawing/Illustrating

You may feel happier with a simple pen or pencil to draw what comes to mind. Again, if you want to, you can add color and shading with different colored pens and pencils. Speak to your art therapist about the type of drawing you want to do and they will be able to help you pick the right set of pens/pencils.

Photography

For some people the simplicity of taking a photograph is more appealing than drawing or painting. Use a camera to capture parts of your life - things you find beautiful, things you wish you could change or even pictures of friends and family. Your art therapist can offer help and advice about the different photography techniques you can use and may also talk you through the development process.

Found Objects

Many artists create art from objects they have found. If you have kept hold of certain objects that feel as if they represent how you feel - try creating a piece of art with them. Turn them into a sculpture, decorate them or simply frame them. If you don't have any objects like this, go for a walk somewhere and work with some objects you find on your way - you may even want to experiment with flower pressing.

Collaging

Collaging is a simple activity that can really help you make sense of your feelings. Cutting out pictures or words and sticking them onto a collage board gives you freedom and will bring out your creative side. Try to pick a theme or emotion you want to explore and make a mood board.

Art Activities

During your art therapy sessions, your therapist may ask you to do certain art activities. These are designed to help you explore your emotions and feelings in a new, creative way. If there is anything you would particularly like to do, be sure to let your therapist know so they can help you. Your art therapist is there to guide you throughout the process, so don't be shy about asking questions if you don't understand the activity.

The types of art activities you will be asked to do will depend on the nature of the issue you are exploring and on the art therapist themselves. Below is a list of examples of the kind of activities you may be asked to do.

Paint your Emotions

Your therapist may give you an emotion to paint (for example, anger) or they may simply ask you to paint the emotion you are feeling then and there. Making use of color and shading can really help to depict certain emotions. It is also important to remember that everyone experiences emotions differently, so don't worry if you're painting looks different to other peoples.

Create an Art Journal

A lot of people find writing in a journal therapeutic, but you may want to keep a visual journal instead. Fill your journal with drawing or scribbles about how you're feeling and try to draw something every day. This will help you to keep in touch with your feelings and will prompt you to consider your actions.

Make a Mandala

A mandala is a circular meditative symbol that is found in many Eastern religions. Take a look at examples and then create your own either drawn in sand or on paper. You may then want to use your mandala as something to meditate on, or you may want to frame it somewhere in your house so you can look at it when you need a moment of calm.

Paint in The Dark

Not worrying about how your picture looks can be incredibly liberating. Painting in the dark allows you to paint from the heart and adds an element of fun. Seeing how everyone's paintings look when the lights go on can also be a wonderful moment.

Draw in the Sand

Drawing shapes and pictures in the sand can be very therapeutic - which is why Japanese Zen gardens often incorporate patterns in the sand. Use your fingers or some tools to create patterns and then simple clear the pattern and start again when you want. You may even want to get yourself a small Zen garden so you can make patterns when you need to calm yourself down.

Draw Something Big

Using your entire body to draw something can help to relieve stress and tension. Experiment with different tools and methods of painting on big canvasses until you find something you like. Once you've drawn something large - why not draw something very small? The subjects of your large and small drawings may reveal something undiscovered about yourself.

Draw a Self-portrait

Self-portraits and portraits of others are common subjects within art therapy. You may simply be asked to draw a self-portrait of what you see when you look in the mirror, or you may be asked to draw another version of yourself.

Paint Someone you've Lost

If you have lost someone close to you, it can often be cathartic to remember them through art. Bringing happy memories to life with a painting or sculpture can give you closure and something to remember them by.

Create a Calming Collage

Collages are great because they are so easy to do. A common art activity is to create a calming collage full of images, colors and words that relax you. This can be used whenever you feel the need to get away from everything, offering a brief window of escapism.

Draw a Visual Autobiography

Drawing your autobiography helps you to look back in a non-confrontational way. Draw happy moments, sad moments and all those other moments in-between to see how they've shaped you. Your art therapist may then ask you to continue this drawing into the future - drawing what you want to happen after therapy.

Paint your Dreams

The dreams we have at night can be surreal and may make no sense at the time. Painting or drawing them can help you understand the symbolism behind them and provides you with a unique and unusual subject matter.

Work on a Group Project

Working with other people can help to develop teamwork and communication skills. It also helps to open your eyes to other people's experiences and may help you to come up with more creative ideas.

Benefits of Art Therapy

There are many potential benefits to art therapy, including but not limited to the following:

- Stress reduction
- Increased sense of self-awareness
- Greater sense of control
- Increased sense of independence
- Improvements in communication
- Healthier, more positive body image
- Improvements in social skills
- Safe expression of difficult emotions
- Increased self-esteem
- Increased problem-solving skills
- Reduced anxiety
- Improved mood
- Improved coping skills
- Healing from trauma
- A greater sense of connection (group art therapy)
- Enhance sense of personal empowerment

Perhaps one of the greatest benefits of art therapy is that it allows individuals to express things that they simply can't put into words. The saying that "a picture is worth a thousand words" is particularly apt with regards to art therapy. Sometimes a drawing or painting is much more powerful and revealing than fifty minutes of dialogue.

Another salient benefit of art therapy is that many individuals feel much more comfortable in art therapy than traditional psychotherapy. Sitting across from and talking face-to-face with a therapist can feel threatening and difficult for some people. Creating art, on the other hand, may help them lower their guard, which helps facilitate the therapy process.

Disorders, Issues, and Conditions that Can Benefit From Art Therapy

Art therapy has been used to benefit a wide range of mental health symptoms and disorders, challenging life issues, and physical health conditions as well. These include the following:

- Depression
- Bipolar disorder
- Anxiety
- Panic disorder
- Schizophrenia and other psychotic disorders
- Eating disorders (e.g. anorexia, bulimia)
- Drug or alcohol abuse and addiction
- Trauma (e.g. survivors of sexual or physical abuse, natural disasters)
- PTSD (posttraumatic stress disorder)
- Compulsive gambling
- Sex addiction
- Autism spectrum disorders
- Dementia
- Traumatic brain injury
- Domestic violence
- Chronic or terminal health issues
- Coping with disability
- Cancer
- Family conflict

- Grief and loss
- Suicidal thoughts
- Individuals with learning problems

Dance Therapy

Dance/movement therapy, usually referred to simply as dance therapy or DMT, is a type of therapy that uses movement to help individuals achieve emotional, cognitive, physical, and social integration. Beneficial for both physical and mental health, dance therapy can be used for stress reduction, disease prevention, and mood management. In addition, DMT's physical component offers increased muscular strength, coordination, mobility, and decreased muscular tension. Dance/movement therapy can be used with all populations and with individuals, couples, families, or groups. In general, dance therapy promotes self-awareness, self-esteem, and a safe space for the expression of feelings.

Principles of Dance Therapy

DMT sessions often include observation, assessment, warm-ups, interventions, verbal processing, and warm-down phases focused on closure. Sessions can be highly structured or non-directive and may be conducted individually or in groups. Although each dance/movement therapist will have his or her own style, certified dance/movement therapists adhere to the following mission and theoretical principles:

Mission

- Facilitate life-span development.
- Prevent, diagnose, and treat issues that interfere with healthy functioning.

- Assess, evaluate, and develop treatment goals.
- Implement planned interventions.
- Develop and adjust treatment to continuously meet the needs of the client.

Key Principles

- Body and mind are interconnected so that a change in one impacts the other.
- Movement can express aspects of the personality.
- Part of the therapeutic relationship is communicated through non-verbal means.
- Movements can be symbolic and can represent unconscious material/processes.
- Movement improvisation/experimentation can bring about new ways of being

Difference between Dance Therapy and Regular Dancing

Most people understand that dancing can be good for their health; it improves cardiovascular endurance, muscle tone, balance, and coordination. Dance can also boost a person's mood, improve his or her body image, and provide an opportunity for fun that may lower overall stress and anxiety. While these elements are certainly beneficial, dance/movement therapy takes therapeutic dance to another level.

People in treatment with a qualified dance therapist have the right to confidentiality, and dance therapists provide a safe space for people to express themselves. Movement becomes more than exercise—it becomes a language. People in treatment communicate conscious and unconscious feelings through dance, which allows a therapist to respond in kind. Dance therapists help people work on issues through the use of a "movement vocabulary" that is centered around physical expression instead of words.

Dance/movement therapists assess body language, non-verbal behaviors, and emotional expressions. Treatment interventions are tailored to address the needs of certain populations. Some intervention examples may include:

- Utilizing "mirroring" (matching/echoing the person's movements) to illustrate empathy for an individual and validation of his or her experience.
- Incorporating jumping rhythms into a dance with a group of people experiencing depression because research has shown decreased levels of vertical movement in people with depression.
- Making use of a "movement metaphor" to help a person physically demonstrate a therapeutic challenge or achievement (e.g. the therapist gives the person in treatment a white flag prop to help him or her celebrate an emotional surrender).

Issues that Dance Therapy Helps with

Dance therapists work with people in therapy to help them improve their body image and self-esteem. Dance/movement therapy is a versatile form of therapy founded on the idea that motion and emotion are interconnected. The creative expression of dance therapy can bolster communication skills and inspire dynamic relationships. It is commonly used to treat physical, psychological, cognitive, and social issues such as:

Physical Issues

- Chronic pain
- Childhood obesity
- Cancer
- Arthritis
- Hypertension
- Cardiovascular disease

Mental Health Issues

- Anxiety
- Depression
- Disordered eating
- Poor self-esteem
- Posttraumatic stress

Cognitive Issues

- Dementia
- Communication issues

Social Issues

- Autism
- Aggression/violence
- Domestic violence trauma
- Social interaction
- Family conflict

Narrative Therapy

Narrative therapy helps people see themselves as separate from their problems and to use their own inherent strengths and abilities to change their lives. The goal of this therapeutic approach is to help them rewrite the negative story – the problem-saturated narrative – that has been dominating their lives for so long. They learn to regard problems as something they *have*, not something they *are*.

In narrative therapy, the therapist isn't the expert; the client is. This shift in perspective from more traditional forms of therapy can be especially empowering for individuals who seek treatment. It's not uncommon for therapy clients to regard themselves – at least to some degree – as weak, inferior, or even damaged because of their depression, anxiety, relationship struggles, unresolved grief, or whatever disorder or challenge that caused them to seek professional help in the first place. Narrative therapists work in collaboration with clients to help them achieve their therapeutic goals in a respectful, non-judgmental, and non-blaming manner.

As clients learn to externalize their problems or challenges and deconstruct the problematic story, they can then begin the process of reconstructing it. They use positive alternatives to create a winning story. It's akin to a writer going back through a novel he's written – one that was rejected by potential publishers due to flaws in the storyline. Building upon the strengths and most interesting aspects of the original story, he rewrites the novel and turns it into a bestseller.

Narrative Therapy Techniques

Following are some of the techniques often used in narrative therapy:

Externalizing the problem – As mentioned above, in narrative therapy, problems are viewed as something people have, not something they are. In other words, people's problems don't define them, nor does their story need to limit or confine them to an undesirable reality. Externalization may involve objectifying, personifying, or labeling the problem – making it a separate or external entity. For example, a person with OCD could personify the intrusive thoughts as an annoying bully.

Mapping the problem – This narrative technique involves the therapist's use of questions that help people identify how a problem is impacting their life. For example, the therapist might ask someone who's feeling stuck in unresolved grief, "What sorts of problems does this grief cause in your life?" Such a question can help him consider things he can do – ways to change the grief narrative – to exert control and reduce its impact.

Identifying unique outcomes – When clients tell their stories, they typically emphasize all the things that support it. For example, the middle-aged man who perceives himself as a failure in life will tell a story that supports his negative story. He'll inevitably gloss over or omit all the successes he's had over the years. The therapist, however, will ask him about exceptions to his narrative. The exceptions, or "unique outcomes," refer to times when the problem wasn't so bad or noticeable. Unique outcomes reveal clients' strengths and skills. Clients can then incorporate these into their new, more positive, narrative.

Deconstructing the story/Identifying alternative narratives – As clients begin to tell their story, the narrative therapist will point out certain things, such as exceptions (mentioned above) to the dominant story, hidden meanings, and potential alternatives to the current storyline. The therapist's observations help clients deconstruct their story and consider ways it can be changed.

Exploring and considering alternative plots or endings helps clients begin the process of rewriting – or *reconstructing* the current, problematic narrative. The new story – which is a more positive perspective of the problem – helps the client begin to overcome it. This process helps clients discover solutions they may not have considered before.

What to Expect in Narrative Therapy

Narrative therapy, like most other types of psychotherapy, usually involves weekly sessions with the therapist. Although the therapist will facilitate the process, it is a collaborative effort between client and therapist. Since clients are regarded as the expert in their own lives in narrative therapy, they – and not the therapist – identify their problems. During sessions, narrative therapists guide the conversation in a way that fosters discovery, and allows and encourages new stories – and new meanings – to emerge. They help their clients rewrite the dominant story – the one that led them to seek therapy – and create one that is much more positive, desirable and empowering.

Disorders, Problems, and Conditions that can Benefit from Narrative Therapy

Narrative therapy can be used to help children, adolescents, adults, and seniors. It can be a very beneficial form of therapy for couples and families. It's also been used effectively in group settings.

The problems and disorders that may benefit from this particular therapeutic approach include, but aren't necessarily limited to, the following:

- Family conflict
- Marital problems
- Relationship issues
- Anxiety
- Depression
- Bipolar disorder
- PTSD
- Recovery from abuse and other types of trauma
- Grief and loss
- OCD
- ADHD
- Substance abuse and addiction
- Anger issues
- Aggressive behavior
- Acting out/tantrums
- Problems at school
- Specific phobias
- Social anxiety
- Lack of confidence
- Low self-esteem
- Sexual identity issues
- Poor coping skills in children and teens
- Eating disorders
- Domestic violence issues
- Chronic illness

Benefits and Advantages of Narrative Therapy

Following are just a few of the many potential benefits and advantages of narrative therapy:

- It's a non-pathological, non-blaming, non-judgmental approach to therapy that separates the problem from the person.
- It regards the client – rather than the therapist – as the expert in his or her own life. This can be very empowering to therapy clients, as many people seek therapy regarding themselves as "broken" or "disordered" and perceiving the therapist as the person who (hopefully) can "fix" them.
- It focuses on the client's strengths, skills, and knowledge rather than on his or her weaknesses and past failures.
- It helps clients look at their problem(s) from a more objective perspective. This objectivity enables them to consider alternative interpretations of their story.
- It can be used to enhance other types of therapy, such as art therapy, play therapy with children. Or family systems therapy.
- The process of externalizing problems and viewing them as separate from the client, therapy clients often feel less guarded and defensive. This enables them to engage more openly and proactively in the therapy process.
- The approach is very optimistic and even playful at times, making it an appealing therapy for anyone who's been in therapy in the past and left feeling disillusioned or discouraged by the process.

Music Therapy

Music therapy—a type of expressive arts therapy that uses music to improve and maintain the physical, psychological, and social well-being of individuals—involves a broad range of activities, such as listening to music, singing, and playing a musical instrument.

This type of therapy is facilitated by a trained therapist and is often used in hospitals, rehabilitation centers, schools, correctional facilities, nursing homes, and hospices.

Music has been used as a therapeutic tool for centuries and has been shown to affect many areas of the brain, including the regions involved in emotion, cognition, sensation, and movement. This fact, combined with the engaging nature of music and the diversity of music forms, makes music uniquely effective in the treatment of a wide array of physical and mental problems, including depression, anxiety, and hypertension.

When traveling music groups played for hospitalized veterans during and after both World Wars, doctors and clinicians began to realize the powerful effects that music has on the healing process and requested that professional musicians be hired by the hospitals. This created a need for specialized training in the appropriate delivery of music as a therapeutic method.

Gradually, colleges and universities began to include music therapy as part of their curriculum, beginning with Michigan State University in 1944. In 1950, the first major professional organization for music therapists was formed, and it became known as the National Association for Music Therapy (NAMT). In 1998, the American Music Therapy Association (AMTA) was formed out of a merger between the NAMT and the American Association for Music Therapy. The AMTA focuses on increasing awareness of and access to music therapy services while promoting the advancement of education, training, professional standards, and research in the field of music therapy.

Music Therapy Session

The intervention methods employed in music therapy can be roughly divided into active and receptive techniques. When a person is making music, whether by singing, chanting, playing musical instruments, composing, or improvising music, that person is using active techniques. Receptive techniques, on the other hand, involve listening to and responding to music, such as through dance or the analysis of lyrics. Active and receptive techniques are often combined during treatment, and both are used as starting points for the discussion of feelings, values, and goals.

Music therapy can be conducted with individuals or in groups, and the music may be chosen by the therapist or by the person in therapy. A music therapist will generally ensure the type and mode of the chosen form of music, as well as the timing of the music intervention, are appropriate for meeting the needs and goals of the individual in therapy.

When introducing music, therapists often base their selections on the Iso principle, which states music is more likely to have influence if it matches an individual's current condition. Therapists therefore try to ensure the lyrics and melody of a selected piece of music are well matched with the mood and psychological state of the person in therapy.

Songwriting is commonly used in music therapy and may involve writing original songs or modifying existing ones, with the latter being a more structured approach to writing. A person might modify a song by changing some of the words or lines, adding new verses, or writing entirely new lyrics to match the existing tune. In cases when songs are freely composed, the therapist may provide an emotion or topic to serve as a starting point.

Music therapy can be used in a variety of ways:

- When a person experiences difficulty communicating after a stroke, singing words or short phrases set to a simple melody can often enhance speech production and fluency.
- A person with impaired motor skills might improve fine motor skills by playing simple melodies on a piano or tapping out a rhythm on drum pads. Listening to a rhythmic stimulus, such as a metronome, can also help a person initiate, coordinate, and time their movements.
- A therapist might play a piece of music for children with autism who have limited social skills and ask them to imagine the emotional state of the person who created the music or the person who is playing it. Doing so can help a person with autism develop or strengthen the ability to consider the emotions others are experiencing.
- Group drumming circles have been used to induce relaxation, provide an outlet for feelings, and foster social connectedness among members of a group. Group members might sit in a circle with a hand drum while the therapist leads them in drumming activities that may involve group members drumming one at a time or all at once. Those who are part of the circle may be asked to express how they feel by playing a rhythm on their drum or the group might be asked to improvise music as a means of increasing group cohesiveness.
- Music might be incorporated into guided imagery or progressive muscle relaxation techniques to enhance the effectiveness of these methods.

Training For Music Therapists

Those wishing to become a music therapist must have at least a bachelor's degree in music therapy from an institution approved by the American Music Therapy Association (AMTA). Music therapy programs involve coursework as well as an internship in an educational and/or health care facility. After successfully completing one of the AMTA-approved programs, individuals must take the national examination offered by the Certification Board for Music Therapists (CBMT). If they are successful in the examination, they receive the credential Music Therapist-Board Certified (MT-BC), which is required for professional practice. Board certification is renewed every five years, and in order to maintain this credential, music therapists must retake the

CBMT examination or complete 100 recertification credits within each five-year period.

Who Can Benefit From Music Therapy?

Music therapy can benefit many individuals. The diverse nature of music means it can be applied in the treatment of concerns both physical and psychological. In some instances, the therapeutic use of music has been able to help people in ways that other forms of therapy have not, as it can sometimes elicit responses that may not appear through more traditional forms of treatment. When people find it difficult to express themselves verbally, they may display a greater degree of interest and engagement in music therapy than they would in a more traditional form of therapy. No background in music is required for a person to benefit from this approach.

Because music can evoke positive emotions and stimulate reward centers in the brain, music therapy is often able to alleviate symptoms of mental health concerns such as:

- Depression
- Mood-related concerns
- Anxiety
- Schizophrenia
- Substance dependency
- Autism
- Personality issues
- Insomnia
- Dementia

Music therapy can both assess and enhance cognitive, social, emotional, and motor functioning, and studies have shown positive results among individuals who have intellectual or physical difficulties, brain injuries, or Alzheimer's. This type of therapy has also been used in the treatment of physical ailments such as cancer and hypertension.

The positive effects of music therapy are not limited to those coping with severe or long-lasting physical and psychological problems, and this therapy can benefit people in a variety of situations. Music is frequently used to reduce stress levels and pain perception among mothers in labor and has been associated with improvements in self-esteem, self-concept, verbal communication, pro-social behavior, socialization skills, group cohesion, and coping skills.

Multitheoretical Psychotherapy

Multitheoretical psychotherapy (MTP) is a new approach to integrative psychotherapy developed by Jeff E. Brooks-Harris and his colleagues at the University of Hawaii at Manoa. MTP is organized around five principles for integration:

1. Intentional
2. Multidimensional
3. Multitheoretical
4. Strategy-based
5. Relational

Being *intentional* involves making informed choices about the focus of treatment, theoretical conceptualization, intervention strategies, and relational stances.

MTP encourages counselors to think in a *multidimensional* manner, recognizing the rich interaction between thoughts, actions, and feelings within the context of biology, interpersonal patterns, social systems, and cultural contexts.

MTP uses a *multitheoretical* framework to organize training and treatment. Psychotherapists can use a combination of theories to formulate a multitheoretical conceptualization to understand clients and guide interventions. The combination of theorical ideas and interventions is based on the individual needs of clients.

MTP encourages therapists to work interactively with thoughts, actions, and feelings:

- Cognitive strategies are used to encourage functional thoughts
- Behavioral interventions promote effective actions
- Experiential-humanistic skills can be used to explore adaptive feelings and personal experiences

Counselors are also encouraged to use theories that explore contextual dimensions that shape thinking, acting, and feeling

- Bio psychosocial strategies focus on biology and result in adaptive health practices
- Psychodynamic-interpersonal interventions are used to understand and modify interpersonal patterns
- Systemic-constructivist skills are used to explore family and social systems and encourage adaptive personal narratives

- Multicultural-feminist strategies encourage clients to adapt to cultural contexts and overcome oppression

MTP training involves building a repertoire of key strategies drawn from different theoretical approaches. Key strategies have been described using strategy markers (suggesting when a particular skill will be most useful) and expected consequences (predicting the likely outcome of a specific intervention). Training also involves learning how to combine ideas and strategies from different theories based on the individual needs of clients. Integrative treatment planning involves conducting a multidimensional survey, establishing an interactive focus on two or three dimensions, formulating a multitheoretical conceptualization, and choosing intervention strategies corresponding to focal dimensions. The Brooks-Harris (2008) text describes applications of MTP to depression, anxiety, substance abuse, and health problems.

As a second-generation model of integrative psychotherapy, MTP combines features of earlier approaches. Like Arnold Lazarus' multimodal therapy, MTP encourages attention to the interaction of different dimensions. Like Prochaska and DiClemente's transtheoretical model, MTP describes the relationship between several different theories. Like Larry E. Beutler's Systematic Treatment Selection, MTP predicts when particular strategies will be most useful.

Emotional Therapy

Emotion-focused therapy (EFT) is a therapeutic approach based on the premise that emotions are key to identity. According to EFT, emotions are also a guide for individual choice and decision making. This type of therapy assumes that lacking emotional awareness or avoiding unpleasant emotions can cause harm. It may render us unable to use the important information emotions provide.

Therapists qualified in EFT can help people seeking assistance with a range of concerns.

These therapists may help people learn to become more aware of their emotions. EFT also allows people to become better at using information provided by adaptive emotions. People may be better able to cope with and decrease negative effects of maladaptive emotions.

Emotion-Focused Therapy Theory

In this approach to treatment, the therapist and the person in therapy collaborate in an active process. Both are viewed as equal contributors. The person in treatment, not the therapist, is seen as the person most capable of interpreting their emotional experience.

EFT is founded in the idea that emotions should be used to guide healthy, meaningful lives. Its theory is based on a scientific inquiry into the human emotional experience. Scientific study of human emotion has provided information about:

- How emotions are produced
- The importance of emotions to human functioning
- How emotions are related to thought and behavior

Emotion schemes is the core concept of EFT. It was developed largely from these theories of human emotion. Emotion schemes are models that outline how emotion can:

- Be experienced physically
- Cause physiologic changes
- Influence thinking
- Guide future action

EFT helps people both accept and change their personal emotion schemes.

Techniques Used in Emotion-Focused Therapy

EFT sessions typically center around the development of two key skills. These are:

1. Arriving at one's emotions through increased awareness and acceptance.
2. Learning to transform emotions and better use the information they provide to avoid negative or harmful behaviors or other effects of certain emotions.

Therapists practicing this method take a compassionate, non-judgmental, and reflective approach to listening and questioning. This allows the person in therapy come to a better understanding of their emotions. Then, various therapeutic techniques known as emotion coaching are utilized. These help people learn new ways to use healthy emotions to guide their actions. Emotion coaching may further help people transform and move on from challenging emotions.

Initial sessions of therapy focus on helping people arrive at emotions. One or more of the following goals are often included in each session:

- Become more aware of emotions
- Learn to welcome, allow, and regulate emotions
- Learn to describe emotions clearly and in detail
- Increase awareness of the multiple layers of emotional experiences and learn to identify the most direct reaction

The next phase of treatment focuses on leaving. It may include the following goals:

- Evaluate whether emotions are helpful or unhelpful in various situations
- Learn to use helpful emotions to guide action
- Identify the source of unhelpful emotions
- Learn to change unhelpful emotions
- Develop alternative, healthy ways of coping with situations that often elicit maladaptive emotions
- Form personal scripts that help challenge the destructive thoughts that may be associated with unhelpful or maladaptive emotions

EFT is generally thought to have been successful when the person in treatment has an increased awareness of their emotional experience. They may also have an improved ability to regulate emotions and be better able to transform unhelpful emotions.

How Can Emotion-Focused Therapy Help?

Unsuccessful attempts to control emotions may exacerbate many issues that bring people to therapy. People who experience depression, for example, may spend large amounts of time avoiding situations that lower their mood. People who experience anxiety might often feel debilitated by their attempts to reduce fear and worry. They may try to stay as far away as possible from the people or things that provoke anxiety.

Through EFT, people may come to see their emotions as valuable sources of information instead of painful or difficult states. They may learn to experience, rather than suppress, these emotions. EFT addresses the regulation and impact of emotions. Emotions impact many mental health concerns. Due to this, EFT may offer benefit in the treatment of many psychological issues.

This method was first used to treat depression. It has since expanded in practice to be used to address:

- Childhood abuse or neglect

- Anxiety
- Eating disorders
- Borderline personality
- Interpersonal issues

EFT has also been found to be potentially effective in working with couples in distress.

Family Therapy

Family therapy is a form of psychotherapy that seeks to reduce distress and conflict by improving the systems of interactions between family members. While family therapists often seek to have all family members (affected by the problem) in the room, that is not always possible or necessary. What distinguishes family therapy from individual counseling is its perspective or framework, not how many people are present at the therapy session. This type of counseling views problems as patterns or systems that need adjusting, as opposed to viewing problems as residing in the person, which is why family therapy is often referred to as a "strengths based treatment."

"Family" is defined by the modern family therapist as anyone who plays a long-term supportive role in one's life, which may not mean blood relations or family members in the same household. Family relationships are viewed as important for good mental health, regardless of whether all family members are participating in the therapy. It is an ideal counseling method for helping family members adjust to an immediate family member struggling with an addiction, medical issue or mental health diagnosis. It is also recommended for improving communication and reducing conflict.

Common Reasons for Seeking Family Therapy

- When a child is having a problem such as with school, substance abuse, or disordered eating

- A major trauma or change that impacts the entire family (i.e. relocation to a new house, natural disaster, incarceration of a family member)
- Unexpected or traumatic loss of a family member
- Adjustment to a new family member in the home (i.e. birth of a sibling, adoption, foster children, a grandparent entering the home)
- Domestic violence
- Divorce
- Parent Conflict

Family therapy is a very specialized skill set, and one should seek a therapist who has received both training and credentials qualifying them to perform this type of counseling. All MFT or Marriage Family Therapists are required to do some family counseling as part of their training. Many LCSW (Licensed Clinical Social Workers) are trained in family counseling, but not all. Use the following overview as a guide for selecting the type of family counseling right for you.

Bowenian (Murray Bowen) – This form of family therapy is the best for those who cannot or do not want to bring family members into the therapy room. Bowenian family therapy utilizes two core concepts, triangulation and differentiation. Triangulation involves the natural tendency to divert anxiety or conflict by involving a third party (i.e. a mother complaining to her daughter about her husband). Differentiation has to do with learning to become less emotionally reactive in one's relationships with family members. Strategies such as letter writing are used to decrease levels of emotional reactivity and increase connectedness among family members.

Structural (Salvador Minuchin) – Focuses on reordering the family system according to how the roles and power are distributed amongst family members. Issues of hierarchy are addressed, making sure the parents (or adult caretakers in the home) are in control and work as a team in setting appropriate boundaries for children. The therapist strengthens adult and sibling relationships by "joining" with the family to help make sure no one person or dyad (two people) in the family system have too much power. "Joining" the family may even involve having one or more family members step behind a one-way mirror so that the therapist can point out patterns of interactions amongst other family members.

Systemic (Gianfranco Cecchin-Milan Model) – This model focuses on the meaning behind family member's behaviors and proposes that family communications are happening on an unconscious level. The therapist takes a neutral and distant approach, yet confronts the family with rituals and behaviors that allow family members to attribute different insight and understanding as to why a problem is occurring. Power is not seen as belonging to any one person in the family, but rather to the unconscious "game" that family members participate in to keep a problem going.

Strategic (Jay Haley) – This is a direct and brief family therapy approach, suited to those who want results in a short period of time. In this direct approach, the family therapist prescribes homework meant to change they way family members interact with the person identified as having the "problem" or "symptom". Hierarchies, coalitions and communication systems are assessed, similar to that in the other family counseling approaches. Common techniques used in strategic family therapy are prescribing the symptom to the family (i.e. telling them to yell at each other more) and reframing the family's problem from a negative to a positive one. The therapist takes over authority from the family member who tends to dominate and control family interactions, making it possible to shift patterns of communication in a way that allow for the "holder" of the family's symptom to get better.

Positive Outcomes of Family Therapy

Family therapy can be helpful on many levels. A good course of family therapy helps:

- Develops and maintains healthy boundaries
- Fosters cohesion and communication among family members
- Promotes problem solving through understanding of family patterns and dynamics
- Builds empathy and understanding.
- Reduces family conflict

Person-centered Therapy

Person-centered therapy was developed by Carl Rogers in the 1940s. This type of therapy diverged from the traditional model of the therapist as expert and moved instead toward a nondirective, empathic approach that empowers and motivates the client in the therapeutic process. The therapy is based on Rogers's belief that every human being strives for and has the capacity to fulfill his or her own potential. Person-centered therapy, also known as Rogerian therapy, has had a tremendous impact on the field of psychotherapy and many other disciplines.

Rather than viewing people as inherently flawed, with problematic behaviors and thoughts that require treatment, person-centered therapy identifies that each person has the capacity and desire for personal growth and change. Rogers termed this natural human inclination "actualizing tendency," or self-actualization. He likened it to the way that other living organisms strive toward balance, order, and greater complexity. According to Rogers, "Individuals have within themselves vast resources for self-understanding and for altering their self-concepts, basic attitudes, and self-directed behavior; these resources can be tapped if a definable climate of facilitative psychological attitudes can be provided."

The person-centered therapist learns to recognize and trust human potential, providing clients with empathy and unconditional positive regard to help facilitate change. The therapist avoids directing the course of therapy by following the client's lead whenever possible. Instead, the therapist offers support, guidance, and structure so that the client can discover personalized solutions within themselves.

Person-centered therapy was at the forefront of the humanistic psychology movement, and it has influenced many therapeutic techniques and the mental health field, in general. Rogerian techniques have also influenced numerous other disciplines, from medicine to education.

Six Factors Necessary for Growth

Rogers identified six key factors that stimulate growth within an individual. He suggested that when these conditions are met, the person will gravitate toward a constructive fulfillment of potential. According to Rogerian theory, the six factors necessary for growth are:

1. Therapist-Client Psychological Contact: This first condition simply states that a relationship between therapist and client must exist in order for the client to achieve positive personal change. The following five factors are characteristics of the therapist-client relationship, and they may vary by degree.

2. Client Incongruence or Vulnerability: A discrepancy between the client's self-image and actual experience leaves him or her vulnerable to fears and anxieties. The client is often unaware of the incongruence.

3. Therapist Congruence or Genuineness: The therapist should be self-aware, genuine, and congruent. This does not imply that the therapist be a picture of perfection, but that he or she be true to him- or herself within the therapeutic relationship.

4. Therapist Unconditional Positive Regard (UPR): The clients' experiences, positive or negative, should be accepted by the therapist without any conditions or judgment. In this way, the client can share experiences without fear of being judged.

5. Therapist Empathy: The therapist demonstrates empathic understanding of the clients' experiences and recognizes emotional experiences without getting emotionally involved.

6. Client Perception: To some degree, the client perceives the therapist's unconditional positive regard and empathic understanding. This is communicated through the words and behaviors of the therapist.

References

- Psychotherapy, patients-families: psychiatry.org, Retrieved 19 May 2018
- Dance-movement-therapy, learn-about-therapy, types: Retrieved 10 June 2018
- Narrative-therapy: addiction.com, Retrieved 19 July 2018
- Emotion-focused-therapy, learn-about-therapy, types: Retrieved 30 March 2018
- Family-therapy: healthypsych.com, Retrieved 14 April 2018

Significant Aspects of Counseling

Counseling is aimed at resolving issue of private and professional life and involves planning strategies for stress management, reconciliation, conflict resolution and for improving emotional health. This chapter explores all such aspects of counseling.

Conflict Resolution

Conflict, arguments, and change are natural parts of our lives, as well as the lives of every agency, organization, and nation.

Conflict resolution is a way for two or more parties to find a peaceful solution to a disagreement among them. The disagreement may be personal, financial, political, or emotional.

When a dispute arises, often the best course of action is negotiation to resolve the disagreement.

The goals of negotiation are:

- To produce a solution that all parties can agree to
- To work as quickly as possible to find this solution
- To improve, not hurt, the relationship between the groups in conflict

Conflict resolution through negotiation can be good for all parties involved. Often, each side will get more by participating in negotiations than they would by walking away, and it can be a way for your group to get resources that might otherwise be out of reach.

Reasons for Conflict Resolution

The main goal of negotiation with your opposition is to come to an agreement that benefits all parties.

Some other good reasons to negotiate are:

- To understand more about those whose ideas, beliefs, and backgrounds may be different from your own. In order to resolve a conflict, you'll need to look at the conflict from your opponent's point of view and learn more about this person or group's perspective and motivations.

- To ensure that your relationships with opponents continue and grow. If you make peace with your opponents, you increase your own allies in the community. Successful negotiations pave the way for smooth relationships in the future.
- To find peaceful solutions to difficult situations. Full-blown battles use up resources -- time, energy, good reputation, motivation. By negotiating, you avoid wasting these resources, and you may actually make new allies and find new resources!

Theories and Models

Dual Concern Model

The dual concern model of conflict resolution is a conceptual perspective that assumes individuals' preferred method of dealing with conflict is based on two underlying themes or dimensions: concern for self (assertiveness) and concern for others (empathy).

According to the model, group members balance their concern for satisfying personal needs and interests with their concern for satisfying the needs and interests of others in different ways. The intersection of these two dimensions ultimately leads individuals towards exhibiting different styles of conflict resolution. The dual model identifies five conflict resolution styles/strategies that individuals may use depending on their dispositions toward pro-self or pro-social goals.

Avoidance Conflict Style

Characterized by joking, changing or avoiding the topic, or even denying that a problem exists, the conflict avoidance style is used when an individual has withdrawn in dealing with the other party, when one is uncomfortable with conflict, or due to cultural contexts. During conflict, these avoiders adopt a "wait and see" attitude, often allowing conflict to phase out on its own without any personal involvement. By neglecting to address high-conflict situations, avoiders risk allowing problems to fester or spin out of control.

Yielding Conflict Style

In contrast, yielding, "accommodating", smoothing or suppression conflict styles are characterized by a high level of concern for others and a low level of concern for oneself. This passive pro-social approach emerges when individuals derive personal satisfaction from meeting the needs of others and have a general concern for maintaining stable, positive social relationships. When faced with conflict, individuals with a yielding conflict style tend to harmonize into others' demands out of respect for the social relationship.

Competitive Conflict Style

The competitive, "fighting" or forcing conflict style maximizes individual assertiveness (i.e., concern for self) and minimizes empathy (i.e., concern for others). Groups consisting of competitive members generally enjoy seeking domination over others, and typically see conflict as a "win or lose" predicament. Fighters tend to force others to accept their personal views by employing competitive power tactics (arguments, insults, accusations or even violence) that foster intimidation.

Conciliation Conflict Style

The conciliation, "compromising", bargaining or negotiation conflict style is typical of individuals who possess an intermediate level of concern for both personal and others' outcomes. Compromisers value fairness and, in doing so, anticipate mutual give-and-take interactions. By accepting some demands put forth by others, compromisers believe this agreeableness will encourage others to meet them halfway, thus promoting conflict resolution. This conflict style can be considered an extension of both "yielding" and "cooperative" strategies.

Cooperation Conflict Style

Characterized by an active concern for both pro-social and pro-self behavior, the cooperation, integration, confrontation or problem-solving conflict style is typically used when an individual has elevated interests in their own outcomes as well as in the outcomes of others. During conflict, cooperators collaborate with others in an effort to find an amicable solution that satisfies all parties involved in the conflict. Individuals using this type of conflict style tend to be both highly assertive and highly empathetic. By seeing conflict as a creative opportunity, collaborators willingly invest time and resources into finding a "win-win" solution. According to the literature on conflict resolution, a cooperative conflict resolution style is recommended above all others. This resolution may be achieved by lowering the aggressor's guard while raising the ego.

Conflict Resolution Curve

There are many examples of conflict resolution in history, and there has been a debate about the ways to conflict resolution: whether it should be forced or peaceful. Conflict resolution by peaceful means is always a better option. The conflict resolution curve derived from an analytical model offers a peaceful solution by motivating conflicting entities. Forced resolution of conflict might invoke another conflict in future.

Conflict resolution curve (CRC) separates conflict styles into two separate domains: domain of competing entities and domain of accommodating entities. There is a sort of agreement between targets and aggressors on this curve. Their judgments of badness compared to goodness of each other are analogous on CRC. So, arrival of all conflicting entities to some negotiable points on CRC is important before peace building. CRC does not exist (i.e., singular) in reality if the chance of aggression of the aggressor is certain. Under such circumstances it might lead to apocalypse with mutual destruction.

The curve explains why nonviolent struggles ultimately toppled repressive regimes from power and sometimes forced leaders to change the nature of governance. Also, this methodology has been applied to capture the conflict styles in Korean Peninsula and dynamics of negotiation process.

Conflict Management

Conflict management refers to the long-term management of intractable conflicts. It is the label for the variety of ways by which people handle grievances—standing up for what they consider to be right and against what they consider to be wrong. Those ways include such diverse phenomena as gossip, ridicule, lynching, terrorism, warfare, feuding, genocide, law, mediation, and avoidance. Which forms of conflict management will be used in any given situation can be somewhat predicted and explained by the social structure—or social geometry—of the case.

Conflict management is often considered to be distinct from conflict resolution. In order for actual conflict to occur, there should be an expression of exclusive patterns which explain why and how the conflict was expressed the way it was. Conflict is often connected to a previous issue. Resolution refers to resolving a dispute to the approval of one or both parties, whereas management is concerned with an ongoing process that may never have a resolution. Neither is considered the same as conflict transformation, which seeks to reframe the positions of the conflict parties.

The role of culture is not always fully appreciated and must be taken into account. Greater transcultural understanding is critical for global security because it diminishes 'hierarchies' and alienation, and avoids dehumanization of the 'other'.

Counseling

When personal conflict leads to frustration and loss of efficiency, counseling may prove helpful. Although few organizations can afford to have professional counselors on staff, given some training, managers may be able to perform this function. Nondirective counseling, or "listening with understanding", is little more than being a good listener—something every manager should be.

Sometimes simply being able to express one's feelings to a concerned and understanding listener is enough to relieve frustration and make it possible for an individual to advance to a problem-solving frame of mind. The nondirective approach is one effective way for managers to deal with frustrated subordinates and coworkers.

There are other, more direct and more diagnostic, methods that could be used in appropriate circumstances. However, the great strength of the nondirective approach lies in its simplicity, its effectiveness, and that it deliberately avoids the manager-counselor's diagnosing and interpreting emotional problems, which would call for special psychological training. Listening to staff with sympathy and understanding is unlikely to escalate the problem, and is a widely used approach for helping people cope with problems that interfere with their effectiveness in the workplace.

Steps to Resolve Conflict in the Classroom

Step 1: Clarifying and Focusing: Problem Ownership

Negative feelings such as annoyance, anger and discomfort can interfere with understanding exactly what is wrong in situations of confrontation and how to set things right again. Gaining a bit of distance from negative feelings is exactly what such moments call for, especially on the part of the person with (presumably) the greatest maturity. *Problem ownership* is defined as deciding who should take ownership of the behavior or conflict in the issue. The main person who is bothered by the root problem is also the "owner" of the problem, and thus the owner of a problem needs to be the one who takes primary responsibility for solving the issue. Identifying ownership makes a difference in how behavior is dealt with, as well as how the problem is effectively solved. It is important to ask clarifying questions to really understand the root causes of the conflict.

Step 2: Active Listening

Several strategies help with distinguishing who has a problem with a behavior and who takes ownership. One of those strategies is active listening. Active listening is attending carefully to all aspects of what a student says and attempting to understand or empathize as much as one can. Active listening consists of continually asking questions in order to test your understanding. It also requires giving encouragement to the student by letting them tell their story, and paraphrasing what the student says so you can form an unbiased conclusion. It is key not to move too quickly at solving the problem by just giving advice, instructions, or scolding. Responding too soon with solutions can shut down the student's communication and leave you with inaccurate impressions of the source or nature of the problem.

Step 3: Assertive Discipline and I-messages

Once you, as the teacher, have taken in the student's point of view, form your comments around how the student's behavior affects your role. Your comments should be assertive, emphasize I-messages, and encourage the student to think about the effects of his or her behavior. They should not be passive, apologetic, hostile or aggressive, but matter-of-fact, such as, "Charlie, you are talking while I am talking." The comments should emphasize I-messages that focus on how the behavior is affecting the teacher's teaching and the other students' learning. An example of this would be, "You are making it hard for me to focus on teaching this math lesson." Lastly, you should ask the student more open-ended questions that make him or her think about the consequences of his or her behavior, such as, "How do the other kids feel when you yell in the middle of class?".

- The comments should encourage the student to think about the effects of his or her actions on others—-a strategy that in effect encourages the student to consider the ethical implications of the actions. Instead of simply saying, "When you cut in line ahead of the other kids, that was not fair to them", you can try asking, "How do you think the other kids feel when you cut in line ahead of them?"

Step 4: Negotiation

The first three steps describe desirable ways of handling situations that are specific and last for only a short time. These steps by themselves could potentially not be enough when conflicts persist over extended periods of time. Often it is better to negotiate a solution in these situations. Negotiating is defined as methodically deliberating various options and deciding on one if possible. Even though negotiation demands time and energy, it often demands less time or effort ultimately than continuing to cope with the problem. The results of negotiation can be valuable to everyone involved in the situation. Various experts on conflict resolution have suggested different ways to negotiate with students about problems that are continual. The theories differ in specifics, but typically are generally similar to the steps we previously discussed:

- Determine what the problem is—involves active listening
- Discuss and share possible solutions, consider their efficacy
- Attempt to reach a consensus: Total agreement on the subject will not always be possible, but should be set as your end goal
- Assess the success of the decision: Renegotiation might be necessary

Tips for Resolving Conflict

Listen for What is Felt as well as Said

When you really listen, you connect more deeply to your own needs and emotions, and to those of other people. Listening also strengthens, informs, and makes it easier for others to hear you when it's your turn to speak.

Making Conflict Resolution a Priority

Maintaining and strengthening the relationship, rather than "winning" the argument, should always be your first priority. Be respectful of the other person and their viewpoint.

Focus on The Present

If you're holding on to grudges based on past conflicts, your ability to see the reality of the current situation will be impaired. Rather than looking to the past and assigning blame, focus on what you can do in the here-and-now to solve the problem.

Pick your Battles

Conflicts can be draining, so it's important to consider whether the issue is really worthy of your time and energy. Maybe you don't want to surrender a parking space if you've been circling for 15 minutes, but if there are dozens of empty spots, arguing over a single space isn't worth it.

Be Willing to Forgive

Resolving conflict is impossible if you're unwilling or unable to forgive others. Resolution lies in releasing the urge to punish, which can serve only to deplete and drain your life.

Know When to Let Something go

If you can't come to an agreement, agree to disagree. It takes two people to keep an argument going. If a conflict is going nowhere, you can choose to disengage and move on.

Conflict Resolution Therapy

Conflict resolution therapy is an approach to treatment that seeks to teach people conflict resolution skills. It was designed primarily to help couples. However, it can be used to address conflict in any situation, whether it arises in a family, between friends or romantic partners, at the workplace, or any other situation. Conflict resolution counseling can be effectively applied to professional and personal relationships to help resolve a wide variety of issues. Therapy will not only help in resolving the conflict at hand, but will provide all parties with skills they can apply to other situations in their daily life. The dynamics at play in these conflicts are well-understood, and parties involved are guided through a process in which they will successfully resolve the conflict.

Stress Management

Stress management consists of making changes to your life if you are in a constant stressful situation, preventing stress by practicing self-care and relaxation and managing your response to stressful situations when they do occur.

Our increasingly busy lives cause our minds a lot of stress. Stress is mental tension caused by demanding, taxing or burdensome circumstances. Stress doesn't just affect our mental state and mood; it affects our physical health as well. When we are very stressed, a hormone called cortisol is released into our bloodstream, suppressing the functioning of our immune, digestive and reproductive systems. That is why it is so important to practice stress management in order to keep our minds and bodies healthy.

It's important to note that not all stress is bad. Stress is actually a survival response when our body thinks that it is in danger. That is why our sympathetic nervous system kicks in and makes our heart rate increase and gives us a burst of the energy hormone, adrenaline, so that we can deal with whatever situation is being thrown at us. This is also called our flight or fight response.

The problem is when we deal with constant stress and worry, or when we don't know how to properly manage a stressful situation. That's why stress management is tremendously important for our health, quality of life and relationships.

Models

The generalized models are:

- The emergency response/fight-or-flight response by Walter Cannon (1914, 1932)
- General Adaptation Syndrome by Hans Selye (1936)
- Stress Model of Henry
- Transactional (or cognitive) Stress Model / stress model of Lazarus after Lazarus (1974)
- Theory of resource conservation by Stevan Hobfoll (1988, 1998; Hobfoll & Buchwald, 2004)

Transactional Model

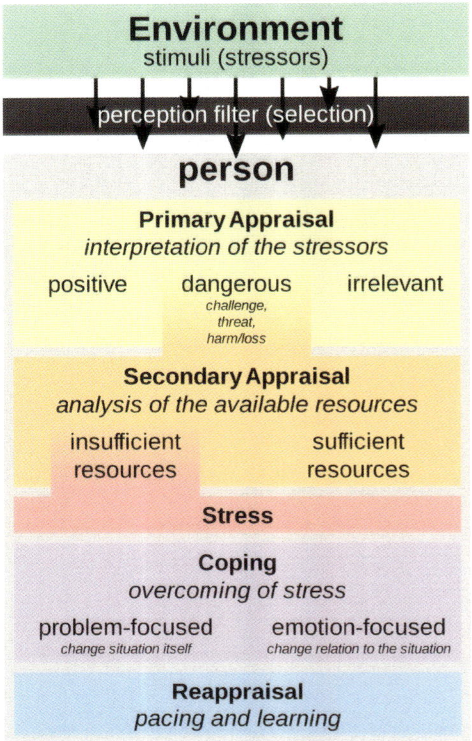

Transactional Model of Stress and Coping of Richard Lazarus

Richard Lazarus and Susan Folkman suggested in 1981 that stress can be thought of as resulting from an "imbalance between demands and resources" or as occurring when "pressure exceeds one's perceived ability to cope". Stress management was developed and premised on the idea that stress is not a direct response to a stressor but rather one's resources and ability to cope mediate the stress response and are amenable to change, thus allowing stress to be controllable.

Among the many stressors mentioned by employees, these are the most common:

- Conflicts in company
- The way employees are treated by their bosses/supervisors or company
- Lack of job security
- Company policies
- Co-workers who don't do their fair share
- Unclear expectations
- Poor communication
- Not enough control over assignments

- Inadequate pay or benefits
- Urgent deadlines
- Too much work
- Long hours
- Uncomfortable physical conditions
- Relationship conflicts
- Co-workers making careless mistakes
- Dealing with rude customers
- Lack of co-operation
- How the company treats co-workers

In order to develop an effective stress management program it is first necessary to identify the factors that are central to a person controlling his/her stress, and to identify the intervention methods, which effectively target these factors. Lazarus and Folkman's interpretation of stress focuses on the transaction between people and their external environment (known as the Transactional Model). The model contends that stress may not be a stressor if the person does not perceive the stressor as a threat but rather as positive or even challenging. Also, if the person possesses or can use adequate coping skills, then stress may not actually be a result or develop because of the stressor. The model proposes that people can be taught to manage their stress and cope with their stressors. They may learn to change their perspective of the stressor and provide them with the ability and confidence to improve their lives and handle all of types of stressors.

Health Realization/Innate Health Model

The health realization/innate health model of stress is also founded on the idea that stress does not necessarily follow the presence of a potential stressor. Instead of focusing on the individual's appraisal of so-called stressors in relation to his or her own coping skills (as the transactional model does), the health realization model focuses on the nature of thought, stating that it is ultimately a person's thought processes that determine the response to potentially stressful external circumstances. In this model, stress results from appraising oneself and one's circumstances through a mental filter of insecurity and negativity, whereas a feeling of well-being results from approaching the world with a "quiet mind".

This model proposes that helping stressed individuals understand the nature of thought—especially providing them with the ability to recognize when they are in the grip of insecure thinking, disengage from it, and access natural positive feelings—will reduce their stress.

Stress Management Tips and Techniques

Count your breaths. This can double as a mini-meditation and be used anywhere. Find a comfortable place to sit (if possible), relax your body, and breathe through your belly while your shoulders relax. Count "one" as you inhale and "two" as you exhale. Then count "three" on your next inhalation, and so forth. This can help you to focus on the present moment, bring your thoughts inward, and relax your body at the same time.

Make a list. Specifically, list things for which you are grateful. Those who feel gratitude tend to feel less stressed in general. By shifting your focus away from what is stressing you right now, you can minimize that feeling of being overwhelmed and remind yourself of the resources you have to manage stress in your life.

Take a walk. By taking even a quick walk, you can give yourself a change of scenery and a little exercise at the same time. Getting your body moving and shifting your focus can give you a quick boost in mood and provide an opportunity to get into a new frame of mind. Both of these things can quickly help you feel less stressed.

Develop Long-Term Stress Relief Habits

Certain habits can promote resilience to stress, as well as increase overall wellness.

For example, those who exercise or meditate regularly tend to become less stressed in the face of a difficult challenge.

It's important to practice at least one of these habits in your daily life as a way to manage your response to the stressors you face. These resilience-promoting practices can not only help you relieve stress as you engage in them, but they can help you to be less reactive to stress that you encounter in your future activities and daily life.

- Meditation: Those who practice meditation once or twice can feel less stressed in minutes. However, those who practice meditation regularly can build resilience toward stress, which helps even more in the long run. Meditation boosts your mood, shifts your focus away from stress, and creates other changes in you that help you to be less reactive to stress. Regular practice also makes meditation easier to engage in when you're feeling overwhelmed, making it more effective when you need it.
- Exercise: You know that exercise is good for your body, but you may forget that exercise is healthy for your stress levels as well. Regular exercise also makes you less reactive to stress and provides you with a useful technique to refocus your attention, let out your frustrations, and even connect with others (say, if you join a class or enlist a workout buddy).
- Self-Care: Taking care of your body is more important than you may realize.

Practicing self-care in the form of getting enough sleep, eating a healthy diet, and staying away from things that aren't good for you (like too much alcohol) can help you stay healthier and happier. You may not realize that lack of sleep can exacerbate stress, but it does. You may not realize that everything seems more stressful if you eat a diet that is too heavy in sugar and does not contain adequate nutrition, but your body will experience this whether or not you make the connection right away. Take care of your body, and see how much less stressed you feel.

Benefits of Stress Management Counseling

- Learn what causes your stress, anxiety or panic and how to regain control
- Discover how to identify stress and anxiety or panic attack triggers and minimize their effect
- Learn how to change automatic thought, behavior and physical symptoms which feed anxiety cycles
- Discover proven, effective panic prevention and removal strategies
- Learn stress reduction techniques to reduce the physical side effects of anxiety or panic
- Develop tailor-made coping strategies to manage stressful situations effectively
- Build a set of techniques and tools that will enable you to effectively prevent or manage any future stress

Reconciliation

Reconciliation counseling offers a divorced/separated parent who has not seen their child (ren) for a period of time, or children who are resisting visits an opportunity to re-connect and re-establish a relationship in a supported, neutral, and safe environment. Custody or access must have been agreed on and/or court ordered.

Trained counselors work separately with the child, the custodial parent, and the non-custodial parent to uncover reasons why there may be resistance. The counselor then works towards re-establishing the relationship, provided it would be in the best interest of the child (ren) to do so. This reconciliation program has had a 72% success rate in helping families move forward with visitation.

Reconciliation or reunification counseling is suited to:

- A parent who has not seen their children for a significant time period

- An estranged parent who has attempted to independently re-establish a relationship with their children several times without success
- An estranged parent who believes he or she has been alienated from their children

Choosing reunification counseling is a prudent means of reconnecting with your children. A meeting between parent and child, particularly after a long separation, is emotionally laden. It is often a frightening time for children who may fear alienating the custodial parent if they begin to accept and enjoy a relationship with the estranged parent.

If the children have witnessed years of arguing and/or familial violence between their parents the estranged parent may become the scapegoat for all that was considered 'bad' in the family home. Without doubt, children have been bitterly disappointed by the breakdown of the family.

The estranged parent may have attempted to re-establish a relationship with their children several times without success. The meetings may have been tense and emotional. There is always the possibility that the children will be questioned when they returned home and the estranged parent further disparaged by the custodial parent. It is obvious that such circumstances will undermine the work underway at my office and significantly hamper any reconciliation between the alienated parent and their children.

Given the fact that the children may be very young, it is important that a psychologist has completed significant education and training in developmental psychology and is licensed to work with a young population as well as adults. Unlike many counselors, a trained psychologist/psychological associate has the necessary expertise to read and understand psychological assessments that may have been completed earlier. As well, it is essential that the psychologist can understand court documents, interact with counsel and the court.

Goals for the program include:

- To restore and/or facilitate a relationship between the estranged parent and the child(ren)

- Uncovering and attempting to resolve the reasons for resistance to visitation
- Assisting the parents to fully understand the needs of each child(ren) and the negative repercussions for the child(ren) of a severed or compromised relationship with a parent
- Correcting the child(ren)'s distortions and replacing these with more realistic perceptions that reflect the child's actual experience with both parents
- Helping each parent to distinguish valid concerns from overly negative views relating to the other parent
- Improving each parent's parenting skills and family communication skills
- Facilitating and monitoring parenting time where appropriate

Emotional Health

Emotional health, a concept synonymous with wellbeing, is vital to living a life of wholeness, balance, and contentment. Simply put, an emotional health definition is one that includes resilience - getting up when life knocks you down. Rather than living a problem-free life emotional health means that one can bounce back from setbacks and thrive despite problems.

Emotional health is an important part of overall health. People who are emotionally healthy are in control of their thoughts, feelings, and behaviors. They are able to cope with life's challenges. They can keep problems in perspective and bounce back from setbacks. They feel good about themselves and have good relationships.

Being emotionally healthy does not mean you are happy all the time. It means you are aware of your emotions. You can deal with them, whether they are positive or negative. Emotionally healthy people still feel stress, anger, and sadness. But they know how to manage their negative feelings. They can tell when a problem is more than they can handle on their own. They also know when to seek help from their doctor.

Mental Health Counseling

Mental Health Counseling is a field of counseling focused on helping patients cope with challenging life events.

How Mental Health Counseling Works

Mental health counseling is a formal, purposeful partnership between a client and a mental health professional. It's sometimes referred to as clinical mental health counseling; not because it's cold and dispassionate but because it is based in sound research and uses techniques proven to be effective.

Counseling is a process of varying lengths during which a mental health counselor and a client work together to explore problems and develop the skills and mind-set needed to transcend challenges and live a life of emotional health. The length of the counseling process varies depending on the individual and the mental health disorder or distress. It can continue anywhere from a few weekly sessions to months or, sometimes, years of occasional sessions.

People seek counseling for many different things. Counseling is for mental illness as well as for specific life stresses, such as a toxic workplace with a bullying boss. Counseling happens individually, in one-on-one sessions with a counselor. Additionally, people can engage in couples therapy, family therapy, or group therapy.

Clinical Mental Health Counseling Approaches

Mental health counselors choose from a plethora of approaches when helping someone. The particular approach used depends on the counselor's professional preference as well as the nature and characteristics of an individual client.

Each approach has a particular focus. Mental health counseling methods can emphasize a person's background, emotions, thoughts, behaviors, or a combination of these elements. Within each category are specific theoretical techniques. Below is a list of the most common approaches, or theories. The list is meant as a starting point for exploration. If there are some methods that resonate with you, you can inquire about theoretical approach when you are searching for a counselor.

Theories Emphasizing Background

- psychoanalysis (Freud and the couch)
- Jungian analytical psychology
- individual (or Adlerian) psychology

Emotion-based Theories

- person-centered (Rogerian) psychology
- existential psychology
- gestalt therapy

Theories Focusing on Thoughts

- cognitive therapy
- rational-emotive behavioral therapy (REBT)

Approaches Emphasizing Behaviors

- cognitive-behavioral therapy (CBT)
- dialectical-behavior therapy (DBT)
- acceptance and commitment therapy (ACT)
- solution-focused brief therapy

A growing counseling approach that falls into the categories of thoughts, feelings, and behavior as well as stands strongly on its own is positive psychology.

Most counselors don't practice one single approach but instead weave together principles of many to best fit individual clients. Approaches most likely to be used on their own include CBT, DBT, ACT, and solution-focused brief therapy.

Benefits of Mental Health Counseling

Counseling indeed helps many people; approximately 80 percent of people in counseling reap benefits. When people engage in mental health counseling, they often gain:

- personal empowerment
- hope
- the overcoming of demoralization caused by social stigma
- acceptance of life
- personal insight
- life skills
- wellness
- prevention of future mental health distress

Mental health counseling improves, and even saves, lives. Seeking counseling is a sign of courage and strength because it's an important step in taking charge of mental health and creating the life that you deserve, a life worth living.

References

- Roberts, Adam; Ash, Timothy Garton, eds. (3 September 2009). Civil Resistance and Power Politics:The Experience of Non-violent Action from Gandhi to the Present. Oxford, UK: Oxford University Press. ISBN 9780199552016
- What-is-stress-management-definition-benefits: study.com, Retrieved 18 March 2018
- de Waal, Frans B. M. (28 July 2000). «Primates—A natural heritage of conflict resolution». Science. American Association for the Advancement of Science. 289 (5479): 586–590. doi:10.1126/science.289.5479.586. ISSN 0036-8075
- Parent-and-child-reconciliation-counselling: pathstonementalhealth.ca, Retrieved 28 May 2018
- «Scheinman Institute on Conflict Resolution – Degrees». Cornell University School of Industrial and Labor Relations. 2014. Retrieved 3 December 2014
- Therapeutic-reconciliation-counselling: connectfamilies.ca, Retrieved 20 June 2018
- Bower, J. E. & Segerstrom, S.C. (2004). «Stress management, finding benefit, and immune function: positive mechanisms for intervention effects on physiology». Journal of Psychosomatic Research. 56 (1): 9–11. doi:10.1016/S0022-3999(03)00120-X. PMID 14987958
- What-is-emotional-health-and-how-to-improve-it, mental-illness-overview: healthyplace.com, Retrieved 17 May 2018
- Mayer, Bernard (27 March 2012). The Dynamics of Conflict: A Guide to Engagement and Intervention (2nd ed.). San Francisco, CA: Jossey-Bass. ISBN 978-0470613535
- Mental-health-keeping-your-emotional-health: familydoctor.org, Retrieved 10 July 2018
- Wahaj, Sofia A.; Guse, Kevin R.; Holekamp, Kay E. (December 2001). «Reconciliation in the spotted hyena (Crocuta crocuta)». Ethology. Wiley-Blackwell. 107 (12): 1057–1074. doi:10.1046/j.1439-0310.2001.00717.x. ISSN 0179-1613
- Mental-health-counseling-how-it-works-benefits, mental-illness-overview: healthyplace.com, Retrieved 19 May 2018
- «Jamia - Centres - Nelson Mandela Centre for Peace and Conflict Resolution - Introduction». Jmi.ac.in. Retrieved 6 December 2014

7

Trauma Counseling and Recovery

Trauma counseling is a kind of psychotherapy aimed at helping people cope with the emotional, physical, cognitive and spiritual responses to loss. Each person has a unique set of emotional responses to the anticipation of loss, or during and after the trauma. This chapter explores the role of trauma counseling for trauma recovery and discusses about the kinds of trauma and the varied trauma treatment techniques.

Trauma

Trauma is the physical, emotional and psychological response when a person experiences high levels of fear or stress without having the chance to escape or mobilise (move away).

Trauma is a stress response that remains frozen in time within the person. When a gazelle is chased in the wild by a lion, the animal experiences stress and fear. The animal may run away, or it may freeze in response to the impending attack. However, when the threat goes away, a gazelle will often run off, or literally shake. This serves the animal as it shakes the stress away.

Our natural response to a threat is to 'mobilise' i.e. to escape it. In some circumstances, a person is unable to avoid a threat and thus experiences high levels of fear and stress, known as trauma.

Animals in the wild will rarely experience trauma symptoms, because animals automatically mobilise through the danger.

Symptoms of Post-traumatic Stress Disorder (PTSD)

PTSD (Post-Traumatic Stress Disorder) arises when a person experiences a threat involving high levels of stress, but they are unable to move through the stress response, meaning they are frozen in the stress response and unable to recognise that the danger has now ceased. PTSD can be recognised by the following symptoms:

- Flashbacks (reliving the trauma as if it were happening now)
- High levels of anxiety and fear
- Avoiding the place where the trauma occurred
- Emotional numbness/disconnection from emotions
- Unexplained physical problems
- Negative self-beliefs such as "I am to blame" or "I am not valuable" or "I am worthless"
- Feeling ashamed
- Suicidal thoughts or behaviours
- Nightmares

How your Childhood Affects your Response to Trauma

A person's ability to come through experiencing a trauma can be grounded in how they learnt to manage their emotions in early childhood. If a person was soothed as a baby, and reassured when they were fearful, this child learns that even though bad things happen, they have the ability to get through them with the support of their parents/guardians.

However, if the child does not have a good enough care giving environment, they may not learn how to regulate emotions and it may be more difficult to overcome the emotions that occur when a threat arises. This does not mean that if you had a good enough care giver, then you will escape PTSD, but it does make prolonged PTSD or complex PTSD less likely.

Coping with Trauma

A survivor of a traumatic event (or series of events) may turn to coping mechanisms in order to deal with the PTSD symptoms. These may include self-harm, alcohol or drug use and other risky behaviours. These are used as a way of regulating emotions that feel too difficult to tolerate. These can be extremely useful as a way of coping with trauma. Coping mechanisms may subside if the trauma begins to be processed.

Many find coping methods such as alcohol, drugs and self-harm to deal with the day-to-day impact of trauma and ptsd. Counseling is a much more effective and safe solution.

Causes of Trauma

As previously mentioned, trauma is subjective and can have a multitude of causes. The common factor for events that lead to trauma is that they are not anticipated and are outside the realms of what we deem to be acceptable - physically, emotionally or socially. Below are some examples of events that could lead to psychological trauma.

Abuse

This can refer to physical, emotional, sexual or verbal abuse. Anything that can be described as improper treatment that leads you to feel violated in some way constitutes abuse. The traumatic event could be a one-off attack or a recurring form of abuse that takes place over long periods of time.

Accidents

Being involved in an accident can lead to a traumatic response. Examples include car accidents, a bad fall and accidentally harming someone else. Even if you were not physically harmed by the accident in question, being involved and experiencing the event can still lead to traumatic feelings.

Brain Tumour and Brain Injury

Injuries and cancer of the brain can be catastrophic for both the person affected and those around them. In some cases, such injuries and illness can alter personalities or affect key motor skills - both of which can lead to symptoms of psychological trauma.

Catastrophic Events

This can relate to natural disasters such as earthquakes, tsunamis and hurricanes as well as man-made events like war and bombings. Being involved in these kinds of events can affect you both directly and indirectly.

Physical Injury

Some physical injuries can change your life forever. You may have had a limb amputated and need to learn to cope with your new disability, or you may be left with physical scarring and chronic pain. Either way, this kind of trauma often requires a great deal of emotional support alongside physical rehabilitation.

Terminal Illness/Bereavement

Whether it's yourself or someone close to you who has been diagnosed with a terminal illness, traumatic symptoms are often experienced. Equally, when someone close to you passes away (whether it's expected or unexpected) you can start to question your belief system and shut down emotionally.

Violence

Experiencing violence in any way can be traumatic. Whether you have been the victim of physical violence, threatened with violence or even witnessed violence - you could find yourself suffering from symptoms of psychological trauma.

Symptoms of Trauma

Symptoms of trauma vary from person to person and depend on the severity of the event. These symptoms can last anything from a couple of days to decades if treatment isn't sought. Some people also find that they do not notice any symptoms immediately after the event as they can often occur some time later.

Common symptoms of psychological trauma include:

- Flashbacks – When you re-experience the traumatic event mentally or physically.
- Insomnia – After a traumatic experience it is common to have difficulties sleeping due to nightmares or due to mentally going over details of the event.
- Anxiety – Feeling constantly anxious after a trauma is very common. Sometimes these feelings turn into anxiety disorders such as PTSD or panic attacks.
- Stress – Even if you handled stress very well before your experience, many people find stress harder to manage after a traumatic event.

- Anger – Feeling angry after a trauma is very common. You might be angry at the person who traumatised you, at the event itself or even at the world. This can lead to outbursts and other anger management issues.
- Depression – Many people fall into a depression after experiencing something very distressing. You can be left wondering why the event happened to you - leading to dark moods and in severe cases, suicidal thoughts.
- Loss of self-esteem – It can be easy to lack self-belief and self-confidence after you have experienced something traumatic. You can be left questioning your identity and what you have to offer the world.
- Self-medication – For some, the only way they feel they can deal with what happened is by self-medicating with alcohol or drugs. This leads to very self-destructive behaviour and can isolate you from friends and family.
- Emotional detachment – For some, the emotions brought up are so severe that they cannot deal with them at all. This can lead to emotional numbness, also known as dissociation. You may refuse to deal with any psychological issues you have and could appear cold and distant to others.

The longer your trauma symptoms go untreated, the more psychological damage they could cause. Therefore it is important to know when to seek professional help.

When to Seek Help

No matter how major or minor your traumatic experience was, you might benefit from professional help from a counselor. As we all react differently to these types of events, it is important not to compare yourself to other people, even if they went through the same experience. By getting help as soon as you need it, you will be giving yourself the best chance to overcome any issues and move on with your life. If you are experiencing any of the symptoms described above and they are persisting for weeks or even months, be sure to seek help.

It is especially important to get help if you experience any of the following:

- You feel unable to function in day-to-day life.
- You are unable to form or maintain relationships.
- You are self-medicating with drugs and/or alcohol.
- You are experiencing severe flashbacks.
- You feel emotionally numb.
- You are suffering from an anxiety/stress disorder due to trauma.

Trauma Treatment Techniques

There are many different treatment options for those going through psychological trauma; the key is finding a treatment that works best for you. Treatments generally involve acknowledging and processing trauma-related memories while releasing any pent up 'fight-or-flight' energy. Learning how to regulate strong emotions and building an ability to trust again is also essential.

The type of treatment you receive will depend on a number of factors, including the kind of trauma you experienced, your personality and your counselor. Following three treatment options are some of the most common when dealing with psychological trauma and are often combined.

Somatic Experiencing

Somatic therapy is a form of body-centered therapy that looks at the connection of mind and body and uses both psychotherapy and physical therapies for holistic healing. In addition to talk therapy, somatic therapy practitioners use mind-body exercises and other physical techniques to help release the pent-up tension that is negatively affecting your physical and emotional wellbeing.

When is It Used

Somatic therapy can help people who suffer from stress, anxiety, depression, grief, addiction, problems with relationships, and sexual function, as well as issues related to trauma and abuse. Those for whom traditional remedies have not been helpful for chronic physical pain, digestive disorders and other medical issues may also benefit from somatic therapy. Somatic therapy techniques can be used in both individual and group therapy settings.

What to Expect

Somatic therapy combines talk therapy with what are sometimes considered alternative forms of physical therapy. The therapist helps you revive memories of traumatic experiences and pays attention to any physical responses you have once the memory is recovered. Physical techniques, such as deep breathing, relaxation exercises, and meditation are then used to help relieve symptoms. Some of the adjunctive physical techniques that may be used with somatic therapy include dance, exercise, yoga, or other types of movement, vocal work, and massage.

How It Works

The theory behind somatic therapy is that the mind, body, spirit, and emotions are all related and connected to each other. As a result, the stress of past emotional and traumatic events affects the central nervous system and can cause changes in the body and even in body language, often resulting in altered facial expressions and posture as well as physical pain. Through developing awareness of the mind-body connection and using specific interventions, somatic therapy helps you to release the tension, anger, frustration and other emotions that remain in your body from these past negative experiences. The goal is to help free you from the stress and pain that is preventing you from fully engaging in your life.

Autonomic Nervous System and Somatic Experiencing Theory

The autonomic nervous system (ANS), which includes the sympathetic nervous system (SNS), the parasympathetic nervous system (PSNS), and the enteric nervous system (ENS), is triggered into action when we're faced with adversity and it governs the fight, flight, or freeze instinct. Although designed to be self-regulating, the ANS can become dysregulated, particularly when full expression of one's response to trauma is repressed. As a result, the body continues to respond as if it is under threat. Somatic experiencing contends that negative symptoms of trauma—such as anxiety, hypervigilance, aggression, and shame—result from denying the body the opportunity to fully process the traumatic event.

Though many people who experience traumatic events recover completely, for those who do not, unresolved trauma can lead to larger mental and physical health concerns, such as posttraumatic stress (PTSD), sleep problems, mood swings, or immune system problems. Somatic Experiencing aims to restore the body's ability to self-regulate in order to achieve balance and integrity.

Method of Somatic Experiencing

Somatic Experiencing sessions involve the introduction of small amounts of traumatic material and the observation of a client's physical responses to that material, such as shallow breathing or a shift in posture. The therapist will frequently check in with the client to assess and record somatic sensations that may be imperceptible to the practitioner, such as feelings of heaviness, tightness, or dizziness. Practitioners proceed carefully and cautiously to avoid retraumatizing or triggering the client, and they help people to develop and employ self-regulating strategies. A key component to enhancing one's ability to self-regulate is the practice of alternating, or "pendulating," between the sensations associated with trauma and those that are a source of strength and comfort.

The SE practitioner will help the client find places of safety, whether that be a place in the body that is not activated by the trauma, or a physical place to retreat to in one's mind. Experiencing the sensations related to the traumatic event in a safe way allows a person to fully process the trauma. Clients also achieve heightened awareness of their physical responses to stress, and this skill can serve them in everyday life.

Cognitive Behavioural Therapy (CBT)

Cognitive behavioral therapy (CBT) is a short-term, goal-oriented psychotherapy treatment that takes a hands-on, practical approach to problem-solving. Its goal is to change patterns of thinking or behavior that are behind people's difficulties, and so change the way they feel. It is used to help treat a wide range of issues in a person's life, from sleeping difficulties or relationship problems, to drug and alcohol abuse or anxiety and depression. CBT works by changing people's attitudes and their behavior by focusing on the thoughts, images, beliefs and attitudes that are held (a person's cognitive processes) and how these processes relate to the way a person behaves, as a way of dealing with emotional problems.

An important advantage of cognitive behavioral therapy is that it tends to be short, taking five to ten months for most emotional problems. Clients attend one session per week, each session lasting approximately 50 minutes. During this time, the client and therapist are work together to understand what the problems are and develop new strategies for tackling them. CBT introduces patients to a set of principles that they can apply whenever they need to, and that'll last them a lifetime.

Cognitive behavioral therapy can be thought of as a combination of psychotherapy and behavioral therapy. Psychotherapy emphasizes the importance of the personal meaning we place on things and how thinking patterns begin in childhood. Behavioral therapy pays close attention to the relationship between our problems, our behavior and our thoughts. Most psychotherapists who practice CBT personalize and customize the therapy to the specific needs and personality of each patient.

Cognitive behavioral therapy was invented by a psychiatrist, Aaron Beck, in the 1960s. He was doing psychoanalysis at the time and observed that during his analytical sessions, his patients tended to have an internal dialogue going on in their minds — almost as if they were talking to themselves. But they would only report a fraction of this kind of thinking to him.

For example, in a therapy session the client might be thinking to herself: "He (the therapist) hasn't said much today. I wonder if he's annoyed with me?" These thoughts might make the client feel slightly anxious or perhaps annoyed. He or she could then respond to this thought with a further thought: "He's probably tired, or perhaps I haven't been talking about the most important things." The second thought might change how the client was feeling.

Beck realized that the link between thoughts and feelings was very important. He invented the term automatic thoughts to describe emotion-filled thoughts that might pop up in the mind. Beck found that people weren't always fully aware of such thoughts, but could learn to identify and report them. If a person was feeling upset in some way, the thoughts were usually negative and neither realistic nor helpful. Beck found that identifying these thoughts was the key to the client understanding and overcoming his or her difficulties.

Beck called it cognitive therapy because of the importance it places on thinking. It's now known as cognitive-behavioral therapy (CBT) because the therapy employs behavioral techniques as well. The balance between the cognitive and the behavioral elements varies among the different therapies of this type, but all come under the umbrella term cognitive behavior therapy. CBT has since undergone successful scientific trials in many places by different teams, and has been applied to a wide variety of problems.

CBT is based on a model or theory that it's not events themselves that upset us, but the meanings we give them. If our thoughts are too negative, it can block us seeing things or doing things that don't fit – that disconfirm – what we believe is true. In other words, we continue to hold on to the same old thoughts and fail to learn anything new.

For example, a depressed woman may think, "I can't face going into work today: I can't do it. Nothing will go right. I'll feel awful." As a result of having these thoughts – and of believing them – she may well ring in sick. By behaving like this, she won't have the chance to find out that her prediction was wrong. She might have found some things she could do, and at least some things that were okay. But, instead, she stays at home, brooding about her failure to go in and ends up thinking: "I've let everyone down. They will be angry with me. Why can't I do what everyone else does? I'm so weak and useless." That woman probably ends up feeling worse, and has even more difficulty going in to work the next day. Thinking, behaving and feeling like this may start a downward spiral. This vicious circle can apply to many different kinds of problems.

Beck suggested that these thinking patterns are set up in childhood, and become automatic and relatively fixed. So, a child who didn't get much open affection from their parents but was praised for school work, might come to think, "I have to do well all the time. If I don't, people will reject me." Such a rule for living (known as a dysfunctional assumption) may do well for the person a lot of the time and help them to work hard.

But if something happens that's beyond their control and they experience failure, then the dysfunctional thought pattern may be triggered. The person may then begin to have automatic thoughts like, "I've completely failed. No one will like me. I can't face them."

Cognitive-behavioral therapy acts to help the person understand that this is what's going on. It helps him or her to step outside their automatic thoughts and test them out. CBT would encourage the depressed woman mentioned earlier to examine real-life experiences to see what happens to her, or to others, in similar situations. Then, in the light of a more realistic perspective, she may be able to take the chance of testing out what other people think, by revealing something of her difficulties to friends.

Clearly, negative things can and do happen. But when we are in a disturbed state of mind, we may be basing our predictions and interpretations on a biased view of the situation, making the difficulty that we face seem much worse. CBT helps people to correct these misinterpretations.

CBT can help you to make sense of overwhelming problems by breaking them down into smaller parts. This makes it easier to see how they are connected and how they affect you. These parts are:

- A Situation - a problem, event or difficult situation. From this can follow:
- Thoughts
- Emotions
- Physical feelings
- Actions

Each of these areas can affect the others. How you think about a problem can affect how you feel physically and emotionally.

All these areas of life can connect like this: 5 Areas

What happens in one of these areas can affect all the others.

There are helpful and unhelpful ways of reacting to most situations, depending on how you think about it. The way you think can be helpful - or unhelpful.

Example

You've had a bad day, feel fed up, so go out shopping. As you walk down the road, someone you know walks by and, apparently, ignores you. This starts a cascade of:

	Unhelpful	Helpful
Thoughts:	He/she ignored me - they don't like me	He/she looks a bit wrapped up in themselves - I wonder if there's something wrong?
Emotional: Feelings	Low, sad and rejected	Concerned for the other person, positive

Physical:	Stomach cramps, low energy, feel sick	None - feel comfortable
Action:	Go home and avoid them	Get in touch to make sure they're OK

The same situation has led to two very different results, depending on how you thought about the situation.

How you think has affected how you felt and what you did. In the example in the left hand column, you've jumped to a conclusion without very much evidence for it - and this matters, because it's led to:

- having a number of uncomfortable feelings
- behaving in a way that makes you feel worse.

If you go home feeling depressed, you'll probably brood on what has happened and feel worse. If you get in touch with the other person, there's a good chance you'll feel better about yourself.

If you avoid the other person, you won't be able to correct any misunderstandings about what they think of you - and you will probably feel worse.

This 'vicious circle' can make you feel worse. It can even create new situations that make you feel worse. You can start to believe quite unrealistic (and unpleasant) things about yourself. This happens because, when we are distressed, we are more likely to jump to conclusions and to interpret things in extreme and unhelpful ways.

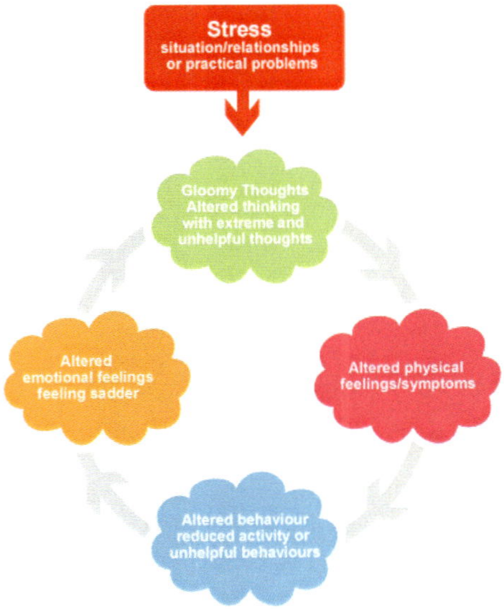

CBT can help you to break this vicious circle of altered thinking, feelings and behaviour. When you see the parts of the sequence clearly, you can change them - and so change the way you feel. CBT aims to get you to a point where you can 'do it yourself', and work out your own ways of tackling these problems.

Types of Cognitive Behavior Therapy

According to the British Association of Behavioural and Cognitive Psychotherapies, "Cognitive and behavioural psychotherapies are a range of therapies based on concepts and principles derived from psychological models of human emotion and behaviour. They include a wide range of treatment approaches for emotional disorders, along a continuum from structured individual psychotherapy to self help material."

There are a number of specific types of therapeutic approaches that involve CBT that are regularly used by mental health professionals. Examples of these include:

- Rational Emotive Behavior Therapy (REBT): This type of CBT is centered on identifying and altering irrational beliefs. The process of REBT involves identifying the underlying irrational beliefs, actively challenging these beliefs, and finally learning to recognize and change these thought patterns.
- Cognitive Therapy: This form of therapy is centered on identifying and changing inaccurate or distorted thinking patterns, emotional responses, and behaviors.
- Multimodal Therapy: This form of CBT suggests that psychological issues must be treated by addressing seven different but interconnected modalities, which are behavior, affect, sensation, imagery, cognition, interpersonal factors and drug/biological considerations.
- Dialectical Behavior Therapy: This type of cognitive-behavioral therapy addresses thinking patterns and behaviors and incorporates strategies such as emotional regulation and mindfulness.

While each type of cognitive-behavioral therapy offers its own unique approach, each centers on addressing the underlying thought patterns that contribute to psychological distress.

Process of Cognitive Behavior Therapy

- During the process of CBT, the therapist tends to take a very active role.
- CBT is highly goal-oriented and focused, and the client and therapist work together as collaborators toward the mutually established goals.
- The therapist will typically explain the process in detail and the client will often be given homework to complete between sessions.
- Cognitive-behavior therapy can be effectively used as a short-term treatment centered on helping the client deal with a very specific problem.

Uses of Cognitive Behavior Therapy

Cognitive behavior therapy has been used to treat people suffering from a wide range of disorders, including:

- Anxiety
- Phobias
- Depression
- Addictions
- Eating disorders
- Panic attacks
- Anger

CBT is one of the most researched types of therapy, in part because treatment is focused on highly specific goals and results can be measured relatively easily.

Compared to psychoanalytic types of psychotherapy which encourage a more open-ended self exploration, cognitive behavior therapy is often best-suited for clients who are more comfortable with a structured and focused approach in which the therapist often takes an instructional role. However, for CBT to be effective, the individual must be ready and willing to spend time and effort analyzing his or her thoughts and feelings. Such self-analysis and homework can be difficult, but it is a great way to learn more about how internal states impact outward behavior.

Cognitive behavior therapy is also well-suited for people looking for a short-term treatment option for certain types of emotional distress that does not necessarily involve psychotropic medication. One of the greatest benefits of cognitive-behavior therapy is that it helps clients develop coping skills that can be useful both now and in the future.

What Does CBT Involve?

The Sessions

You can do CBT individually or with a group of people, or even a self-help book or computer programme.

If you have individual therapy:

- You will usually meet with a therapist for between 5 and 20, weekly, or fortnightly sessions. Each session will last between 30 and 60 minutes.
- In the first 2-4 sessions, the therapist will check that you can use this sort of treatment and you will check that you feel comfortable with it.

- The therapist will also ask you questions about your past life and background. Although CBT concentrates on the here and now, at times you may need to talk about the past to understand how it is affecting you now.
- You decide what you want to deal with in the short, medium and long term.
- You and the therapist will usually start by agreeing on what to discuss that day.

Work

- With the therapist, you break each problem down into its separate parts, as in the example above. To help this process, your therapist may ask you to keep a diary. This will help you to identify your individual patterns of thoughts, emotions, bodily feelings and actions.
- Together you will look at your thoughts, feelings and behaviours to work out:
    - if they are unrealistic or unhelpful.
    - how they affect each other, and you.
- The therapist will then help you to work out how to change unhelpful thoughts and behaviours.
- It's easy to talk about doing something, much harder to actually do it. So, after you have identified what you can change, your therapist will recommend 'homework' - you practise these changes in your everyday life. Depending on the situation, you might start to:
    - question a self-critical or upsetting thought and replace it with a more helpful (and more realistic) one that you have developed in CBT.
    - recognise that you are about to do something that will make you feel worse and, instead, do something more helpful.
- At each meeting you discuss how you've got on since the last session. Your therapist can help with suggestions if any of the tasks seem too hard or don't seem to be helping.
- They will not ask you to do things you don't want to do - you decide the pace of the treatment and what you will and won't try. The strength of CBT is that you can continue to practise and develop your skills even after the sessions have finished. This makes it less likely that your symptoms or problems will return.

Effectiveness of CBT

- It is one of the most effective treatments for conditions where anxiety or depression is the main problem.

- It is the most effective psychological treatment for moderate and severe depression.
- It is as effective as antidepressants for many types of depression.

Other Treatments of CBT

CBT is used in many conditions, so it isn't possible to list them all in this leaflet. We will look at alternatives to the most common problems - anxiety and depression.

- CBT isn't for everyone. Another type of talking treatment may work better for you.
- CBT works as well as antidepressants for many forms of depression. It may be slightly better than antidepressants in helping anxiety.
- For severe depression, CBT should be used with antidepressant medication. When you are very low, you may find it hard to change the way you think until the antidepressants have started to make you feel better.
- Tranquillisers should not be used as a long term treatment for anxiety. CBT is a better option.

Eye Movement Desensitization and Reprocessing (EMDR)

Eye Movement Desensitization and Reprocessing EMDR is a psychotherapy treatment that was originally designed to alleviate the distress associated with traumatic memories Shapiro, 1989a, 1989b. Shapiro's 2001 Adaptive Information Processing model posits that EMDR therapy facilitates the accessing and processing of traumatic memories and other adverse life experience to bring these to an adaptive resolution. After successful treatment with EMDR therapy, affective distress is relieved, negative beliefs are reformulated, and physiological arousal is reduced. During EMDR therapy the client attends to emotionally disturbing material in brief sequential doses while simultaneously focusing on an external stimulus. Therapist directed lateral eye movements are the most commonly used external stimulus but a variety of other stimuli including hand-tapping and audio stimulation are often used Shapiro, 1991. Shapiro 1995, 2001 hypothesizes that EMDR therapy facilitates the accessing of the traumatic memory network, so that information processing is enhanced, with new associations forged between the traumatic memory and more adaptive memories or information. These new associations are thought to result in complete information processing, new learning, elimination of emotional distress, and development of cognitive insights. EMDR therapy uses a three pronged protocol: 1 the past events that have laid the groundwork for dysfunction are processed, forging new associative links with adaptive information; 2 the current circumstances that elicit distress are targeted, and internal and external triggers are desensitized; 3 imaginal templates of future events are incorporated, to assist the client in acquiring the skills needed for adaptive functioning.

EMDR (Eye Movement Desensitization and Reprocessing) is a psychotherapy that enables people to heal from the symptoms and emotional distress that are the result of disturbing life experiences. Repeated studies show that by using EMDR therapy people can experience the benefits of psychotherapy that once took years to make a difference. It is widely assumed that severe emotional pain requires a long time to heal. EMDR therapy shows that the mind can in fact heal from psychological trauma much as the body recovers from physical trauma. When you cut your hand, your body works to close the wound. If a foreign object or repeated injury irritates the wound, it festers and causes pain. Once the block is removed, healing resumes. EMDR therapy demonstrates that a similar sequence of events occurs with mental processes. The brain's information processing system naturally moves toward mental health. If the system is blocked or imbalanced by the impact of a disturbing event, the emotional wound festers and can cause intense suffering. Once the block is removed, healing resumes. Using the detailed protocols and procedures learned in EMDR therapy training sessions, clinicians help clients activate their natural healing processes.

More than 30 positive controlled outcome studies have been done on EMDR therapy. Some of the studies show that 84%-90% of single-trauma victims no longer have post-traumatic stress disorder after only three 90-minute sessions. Another study, funded by the HMO Kaiser Permanente, found that 100% of the single-trauma victims and 77% of multiple trauma victims no longer were diagnosed with PTSD after only six 50-minute sessions. In another study, 77% of combat veterans were free of PTSD in 12 sessions. There has been so much research on EMDR therapy that it is now recognized as an effective form of treatment for trauma and other disturbing experiences by organizations such as the American Psychiatric Association, the World Health Organization and the Department of Defense. Given the worldwide recognition as an effective treatment of trauma, you can easily see how EMDR therapy would be effective in treating the "everyday" memories that are the reason people have low self-esteem, feelings of powerlessness, and all the myriad problems that bring them in for therapy. Over 100,000 clinicians throughout the world use the therapy. Millions of people have been treated successfully over the past 25 years.

EMDR therapy is an eight-phase treatment. Eye movements or other bilateral stimulation are used during one part of the session. After the clinician has determined which memory to target first, he asks the client to hold different aspects of that event or thought in mind and to use his eyes to track the therapist's hand as it moves back and forth across the client's field of vision. As this happens, for reasons believed by a Harvard researcher to be connected with the biological mechanisms involved in Rapid Eye Movement (REM) sleep, internal associations arise and the clients begin to process the memory and disturbing feelings. In successful EMDR therapy, the meaning of painful events is transformed on an emotional level. For instance, a rape victim shifts from feeling horror and self-disgust to holding the firm belief that, "I survived it and I am strong." Unlike talk therapy, the insights clients gain in EMDR therapy result not so much from clinician interpretation, but from the client's own accelerated intellectual and emotional processes. The net effect is that clients conclude EMDR therapy feeling empowered by the very experiences that once debased them. Their wounds have not just closed, they have transformed. As a natural outcome of the EMDR therapeutic process, the clients' thoughts, feelings and behavior are all robust indicators of emotional health and resolution—all without speaking in detail or doing homework used in other therapies.

Phases of EMDR Therapy

1. History taking: The therapist and client review past events, current concerns and future needs, and identify target events for processing.

2. Preparation: To prepare for coping with any distress that may arise during the desensitization phase, the person in therapy selects a safe-place image that can provide stabilization and self-control as needed.

3. Assessment: With the distressing event in mind, the client's negative beliefs about himself or herself are recorded, evaluated, and measured. In contrast, a desirable positive belief is selected, and this belief is measured to determine how true it feels to the client. Physical symptoms are recorded as well.

4. Desensitization: Bilateral stimulation, in the form of eye movements, tones, or taps are used to reprocess the distressing event. The therapist will break periodically to check in on the client's level of disturbance.

5. Installation: The selected positive cognition is the target of the bilateral stimulation in this phase. The therapist will check in periodically to see how true the desired belief feels to the client.

6. Body scan: Any residual physical tension or distress indicates that the event is not fully processed, and the bilateral stimulation continues, if necessary.

7. Closure: This phase will occur at the end of a session, regardless of whether or not the memory is fully processed. A complete sequence of EMDR therapy can take several sessions, and it is important to reach stabilization before the session ends. Closure can include guided imagery or discussion of the session.

8. Re-evaluation: The next session begins here, in order to evaluate and measure the level of disturbance and the accuracy of the targeted positive belief. If the target remains unresolved, the session will resume with desensitization, phase 4.

Treatment

EMDR therapy combines different elements to maximize treatment effects. EMDR therapy involves attention to three time periods: the past, present, and future. Focus is given to past disturbing memories and related events. Also, it is given to current situations that cause distress, and to developing the skills and attitudes needed for positive future actions. With EMDR therapy, these items are addressed using an eight-phase treatment approach.

Phase 1: The first phase is a history-taking sessions. The therapist assesses the client's readiness and develops a treatment plan. Client and therapist identify possible targets for EMDR processing. These include distressing memories and current situations that cause emotional distress. Other targets may include related incidents in the past. Emphasis is placed on the development of specific skills and behaviors that will be needed by the client in future situations.

Initial EMDR processing may be directed to childhood events rather than to adult onset stressors or the identified critical incident if the client had a problematic childhood. Clients generally gain insight on their situations, the emotional distress resolves and they start to change their behaviors. The length of treatment depends upon the number of traumas and the age of PTSD onset. Generally, those with single event adult onset trauma can be successfully treated in under 5 hours. Multiple trauma victims may require a longer treatment time.

Phase 2: During the second phase of treatment, the therapist ensures that the client has several different ways of handling emotional distress. The therapist may teach the client a variety of imagery and stress reduction techniques the client can use during and between sessions. A goal of EMDR therapy is to produce rapid and effective change while the client maintains equilibrium during and between sessions.

Phases 3-6: In phases three to six, a target is identified and processed using EMDR therapy procedures. These involve the client identifying three things:

1. The vivid visual image related to the memory
2. A negative belief about self
3. Related emotions and body sensations.

In addition, the client identifies a positive belief. The therapist helps the client rate the positive belief as well as the intensity of the negative emotions. After this, the client is instructed to focus on the image, negative thought, and body sensations while simultaneously engaging in EMDR processing using sets of bilateral stimulation. These sets may include eye movements, taps, or tones. The type and length of these sets is different for each client. At this point, the EMDR client is instructed to just notice whatever spontaneously happens.

After each set of stimulation, the clinician instructs the client to let his/her mind go blank and to notice whatever thought, feeling, image, memory, or sensation comes to mind. Depending upon the client's report, the clinician will choose the next focus of attention. These repeated sets with directed focused attention occur numerous times throughout the session. If the client becomes distressed or has difficulty in progressing, the therapist follows established procedures to help the client get back on track.

When the client reports no distress related to the targeted memory, they are asked to think of the preferred positive belief that was identified at the beginning of the session. At this time, the client may adjust the positive belief if necessary, and then focus on it during the next set of distressing events.

Phase 7: In phase seven, closure, the therapist asks the client to keep a log during the week. The log should document any related material that may arise. It serves to remind the client of the self-calming activities that were mastered in phase two.

Phase 8: The next session begins with phase eight. Phase eight consists of examining the progress made thus far. The EMDR treatment processes all related historical events, current incidents that elicit distress, and future events that will require different responses.

Trauma Counseling

Counseling meant for helping people to cope up with trauma is known as trauma counseling.

Working with a Values-Based counselor to address the effects of a trauma can be a confusing and frightening task to begin. Whether the events occurred in childhood, five years ago, or last week, the impact of these troubling situations is not something we are taught how to resolve. Often, the thought of going through the events again and seemingly reliving the tragedy may appear more than we can bear. When you work with a counselor who has been professionally trained in the resolution for trauma, he or she understands this apprehension and is committed to working through these issues at whatever pace is comfortable and safe for you.

Many times, we learn how to cope and manage the symptoms of a trauma. Whether this is learning to calm ourselves when we experience a panic attack upon the reminder of an event, or seeking solace in our friends when we experience depression or sadness over the effects of the trauma. While these are important and helpful methods to manage the symptoms, a trauma counselor focuses on resolution of the originating feelings and emotions that require coping skills into the future. If individuals have a lack of safety or security as a result of an event that left them exposed, vulnerable, or violated, trauma counseling begins by establishing a sense of safety for the individual.

The trauma counselor utilizes specialized techniques to identify and work through the emotions that have been internalized from the event. Often, individuals do not think "I should be afraid", rather it becomes a state of being that is used to protect from potential harm. However, when this protection leaves the individual feeling anxious rather than safe, or sad about past events rather than focused on future possibilities, the coping mechanisms lose their usefulness. It is at this point that we see many individuals seek crisis counseling, as the current coping skills are no longer able to manage the symptoms. For some, this collapse of internal coping mechanisms can result in an emotional and psychological breakdown.

References

- What-is-trauma-counselling: thepalmeirapractice.org.uk, Retrieved 21 June 2018
- Somatic-therapy, therapy-types: psychologytoday.com, Retrieved 11 April 2018
- In-depth-cognitive-behavioral-therapy: psychcentral.com, Retrieved 31 March 2018
- What-is-cognitive-behavior-therapy-2795747: verywellmind.com, Retrieved 19 May 2018
- Trauma-counselling: theravive.com, Retrieved 09 March 2018
- Eye-movement-desensitization-and-reprocessing, learn-about-therapy: goodtherapy.org, Retrieved 30 June 2018

Depression and Counseling

Depression is the state of the mind characterized by an aversion to activity and low spirits that adversely affects the behavior, thoughts, feelings, and the sense of well-being. Counseling can play a significant role in the management of depression. The topics elaborated in this chapter explore the impact of counseling on depression through the inclusion of topics related to the types of depression, effective treatment, techniques of depression, etc.

Depression

Depression is a mood disorder that causes a persistent feeling of sadness and loss of interest. Also called major depressive disorder or clinical depression, it affects how you feel, think and behave and can lead to a variety of emotional and physical problems. You may have trouble doing normal day-to-day activities, and sometimes you may feel as if life isn't worth living.

More than just a bout of the blues, depression isn't a weakness and you can't simply "snap out" of it. Depression may require long-term treatment. But don't get discouraged. Most people with depression feel better with medication, psychotherapy or both.

Symptoms

Although depression may occur only once during your life, people typically have multiple episodes. During these episodes, symptoms occur most of the day, nearly every day and may include:

- Feelings of sadness, tearfulness, emptiness or hopelessness
- Angry outbursts, irritability or frustration, even over small matters
- Loss of interest or pleasure in most or all normal activities, such as sex, hobbies or sports
- Sleep disturbances, including insomnia or sleeping too much
- Tiredness and lack of energy, so even small tasks take extra effort
- Reduced appetite and weight loss or increased cravings for food and weight gain
- Anxiety, agitation or restlessness
- Slowed thinking, speaking or body movements
- Feelings of worthlessness or guilt, fixating on past failures or self-blame
- Trouble thinking, concentrating, making decisions and remembering things
- Frequent or recurrent thoughts of death, suicidal thoughts, suicide attempts or suicide
- Unexplained physical problems, such as back pain or headaches

For many people with depression, symptoms usually are severe enough to cause noticeable problems in day-to-day activities, such as work, school, social activities or relationships with others. Some people may feel generally miserable or unhappy without really knowing why.

Depression Symptoms in Children and Teens

Common signs and symptoms of depression in children and teenagers are similar to those of adults, but there can be some differences.

- In younger children, symptoms of depression may include sadness, irritability, clinginess, worry, aches and pains, refusing to go to school, or being underweight.
- In teens, symptoms may include sadness, irritability, feeling negative and worthless, anger, poor performance or poor attendance at school, feeling misunderstood and extremely sensitive, using recreational drugs or alcohol, eating or sleeping too much, self-harm, loss of interest in normal activities, and avoidance of social interaction.

Depression Symptoms in Older Adults

Depression is not a normal part of growing older, and it should never be taken lightly. Unfortunately, depression often goes undiagnosed and untreated in older adults, and they may feel reluctant to seek help. Symptoms of depression may be different or less obvious in older adults, such as:

- Memory difficulties or personality changes
- Physical aches or pain
- Fatigue, loss of appetite, sleep problems or loss of interest in sex — not caused by a medical condition or medication
- Often wanting to stay at home, rather than going out to socialize or doing new things
- Suicidal thinking or feelings, especially in older men.

Causes

The causes of depression are not fully understood and may not be down to a single source. Depression is likely to be due to a complex combination of factors that include:

- genetics
- biological - changes in neurotransmitter levels
- environmental
- psychological and social (psychosocial).

Depression has a wide range of causes and potential treatments.

Some people are at higher risk of depression than others; risk factors include:

- Life events: These include bereavement, divorce, work issues, relationships with friends and family, financial problems, medical concerns, or acute stress.
- Personality: Those with less successful coping strategies, or previous life trauma are more suceptible.
- Genetic factors: Having a first-degree relatives with depression increases the risk.

- Childhood trauma.
- Some prescription drugs: These include corticosteroids, some beta-blockers, interferon, and other prescription drugs.
- Abuse of recreational drugs: Abuse of alcohol, amphetamines, and other drugs are strongly linked to depression.
- A past head injury.
- Having had one episode of major depression: This increases the risk of a subsequent one.
- Chronic pain syndromes: These and other chronic conditions, such as diabetes, chronic obstructive pulmonary disease, and cardiovascular disease make depression more likely.

Difference between Depression and Sadness

Depression is different from Sadness or Grief/Bereavement

The death of a loved one, loss of a job or the ending of a relationship are difficult experiences for a person to endure. It is normal for feelings of sadness or grief to develop in response to such situations. Those experiencing loss often might describe themselves as being "depressed."

But being sad is not the same as having depression. The grieving process is natural and unique to each individual and shares some of the same features of depression. Both grief and depression may involve intense sadness and withdrawal from usual activities. They are also different in important ways:

- In grief, painful feelings come in waves, often intermixed with positive memories of the deceased. In major depression, mood and/or interest (pleasure) are decreased for most of two weeks.
- In grief, self-esteem is usually maintained. In major depression, feelings of worthlessness and self-loathing are common.
- For some people, the death of a loved one can bring on major depression. Losing a job or being a victim of a physical assault or a major disaster can lead to depression for some people. When grief and depression co-exist, the grief is more severe and lasts longer than grief without depression. Despite some overlap between grief and depression, they are different. Distinguishing between them can help people get the help, support or treatment they need.

Types of Depression

1. Major depression, is the most common type of depression. Often, people with major depression experience recurrent episodes throughout their lives.
2. Dysthymia is a persistent low mood over a long period of time, even a year or more. It could be described as feeling like you're living on autopilot.
3. Some people are more sensitive to the lower amount of light in the wintertime. Seasonal Affective Disorder is a type of depression brought on from a lack of natural sunlight.
4. Those with Atypical Depression often report feeling a heaviness in their limbs. They may suffer from irritability and relationship problems, as well as be prone to overeating and oversleeping.
5. Bipolar Disorder is also called Manic Depressive Disorder because it involves alternating between mania and depressive episodes.
6. Sometimes depressive episodes can get so severe that hallucinations or delusions are present, the person becomes catatonic, or they feel stuck in bed. This is known as Psychotic Depression.
7. Postpartum Depression occurs after giving birth. Mothers may feel disconnected from their new baby or fear that they will hurt their child.
8. Severe depression that shows up during the second half of the menstrual cycle is called Premenstrual Dysphoric Disorder. It affects the individual's ability to function normally.
9. Situational Depression is triggered by a life-changing event. It could be anything, from losing your job to the death of an immediate family member.

Treatment of Depression

Medications

- Selective serotonin reuptake inhibitors (SSRIs). Doctors often start by prescribing an SSRI. These drugs are considered safer and generally cause fewer bothersome side effects than other types of antidepressants. SSRIs include citalopram (Celexa), escitalopram (Lexapro), fluoxetine (Prozac), paroxetine (Paxil, Pexeva), sertraline (Zoloft) and vilazodone (Viibryd).

- Serotonin-norepinephrine reuptake inhibitors (SNRIs). Examples of SNRIs include duloxetine (Cymbalta), venlafaxine (Effexor XR), desvenlafaxine (Pristiq, Khedezla) and levomilnacipran (Fetzima).
- Atypical antidepressants. These medications don't fit neatly into any of the other antidepressant categories. They include bupropion (Wellbutrin XL, Wellbutrin SR, Aplenzin, Forfivo XL), mirtazapine (Remeron), nefazodone, trazodone and vortioxetine (Trintellix).
- Tricyclic antidepressants. These drugs — such as imipramine (Tofranil), nortriptyline (Pamelor), amitriptyline, doxepin, trimipramine (Surmontil), desipramine (Norpramin) and protriptyline (Vivactil) — can be very effective, but tend to cause more-severe side effects than newer antidepressants. So tricyclics generally aren't prescribed unless you've tried an SSRI first without improvement.
- Monoamine oxidase inhibitors (MAOIs). MAOIs — such as tranylcypromine (Parnate), phenelzine (Nardil) and isocarboxazid (Marplan) — may be prescribed, typically when other drugs haven't worked, because they can have serious side effects. Using MAOIs requires a strict diet because of dangerous (or even deadly) interactions with foods – such as certain cheeses, pickles and wines – and some medications and herbal supplements. Selegiline (Emsam), a newer MAOI that sticks on the skin as a patch, may cause fewer side effects than other MAOIs do. These medications can't be combined with SSRIs.
- Other medications. Other medications may be added to an antidepressant to enhance antidepressant effects. Your doctor may recommend combining two antidepressants or adding medications such as mood stabilizers or antipsychotics. Anti-anxiety and stimulant medications also may be added for short-term use.

Psychotherapy

Psychotherapy is a general term for treating depression by talking about your condition and related issues with a mental health professional. Psychotherapy is also known as talk therapy or psychological therapy.

Different types of psychotherapy can be effective for depression, such as cognitive behavioral therapy or interpersonal therapy. Your mental health professional may also recommend other types of therapies. Psychotherapy can help you:

- Adjust to a crisis or other current difficulty
- Identify negative beliefs and behaviors and replace them with healthy, positive ones
- Explore relationships and experiences, and develop positive interactions with others

- Find better ways to cope and solve problems
- Identify issues that contribute to your depression and change behaviors that make it worse
- Regain a sense of satisfaction and control in your life and help ease depression symptoms, such as hopelessness and anger
- Learn to set realistic goals for your life
- Develop the ability to tolerate and accept distress using healthier behaviors

Alternate Formats for Therapy

Formats for depression therapy as an alternative to face-to-face office sessions are available and may be an effective option for some people. Therapy can be provided, for example, as a computer program, by online sessions, or using videos or workbooks. Programs can be guided by a therapist or be partially or totally independent.

Before you choose one of these options, discuss these formats with your therapist to determine if they may be helpful for you. Also, ask your therapist if he or she can recommend a trusted source or program. Some may not be covered by your insurance and not all developers and online therapists have the proper credentials or training.

Smartphones and tablets that offer mobile health apps, such as support and general education about depression, are not a substitute for seeing your doctor or therapist.

Hospital and Residential Treatment

In some people, depression is so severe that a hospital stay is needed. This may be necessary if you can't care for yourself properly or when you're in immediate danger of harming yourself or someone else. Psychiatric treatment at a hospital can help keep you calm and safe until your mood improves.

Partial hospitalization or day treatment programs also may help some people. These programs provide the outpatient support and counseling needed to get symptoms under control.

Other Treatment Options

For some people, other procedures, sometimes called brain stimulation therapies, may be suggested:

- Electroconvulsive therapy (ECT). In ECT, electrical currents are passed through the brain to impact the function and effect of neurotransmitters in your brain to relieve depression. ECT is usually used for people who don't get better with medications, can't take antidepressants for health reasons or are at high risk of suicide.

- Transcranial magnetic stimulation (TMS). TMS may be an option for those who haven't responded to antidepressants. During TMS, a treatment coil placed against your scalp sends brief magnetic pulses to stimulate nerve cells in your brain that are involved in mood regulation and depression.

Lifestyle and Home Remedies

Depression generally isn't a disorder that you can treat on your own. But in addition to professional treatment, these self-care steps can help:

- Stick to your treatment plan. Don't skip psychotherapy sessions or appointments. Even if you're feeling well, don't skip your medications. If you stop, depression symptoms may come back, and you could also experience withdrawal-like symptoms. Recognize that it will take time to feel better.
- Learn about depression. Education about your condition can empower you and motivate you to stick to your treatment plan. Encourage your family to learn about depression to help them understand and support you.
- Pay attention to warning signs. Work with your doctor or therapist to learn what might trigger your depression symptoms. Make a plan so that you know what to do if your symptoms get worse. Contact your doctor or therapist if you notice any changes in symptoms or how you feel. Ask relatives or friends to help watch for warning signs.
- Avoid alcohol and recreational drugs. It may seem like alcohol or drugs lessen depression symptoms, but in the long run they generally worsen symptoms and make depression harder to treat. Talk with your doctor or therapist if you need help with alcohol or substance use.
- Take care of yourself. Eat healthy, be physically active and get plenty of sleep. Consider walking, jogging, swimming, gardening or another activity that you enjoy. Sleeping well is important for both your physical and mental well-being. If you're having trouble sleeping, talk to your doctor about what you can do.

Alternative Medicine

Alternative medicine is the use of a nonconventional approach instead of conventional medicine. Complementary medicine is a nonconventional approach used along with conventional medicine — sometimes called integrative medicine.

Make sure you understand the risks as well as possible benefits if you pursue alternative or complementary therapy. Don't replace conventional medical treatment or psychotherapy with alternative medicine. When it comes to depression, alternative treatments aren't a substitute for medical care.

Mind-body Connections

Integrative medicine practitioners believe the mind and body must be in harmony for you to stay healthy. Examples of mind-body techniques that may be helpful for depression include:

- Acupuncture
- Relaxation techniques such as yoga or tai chi
- Meditation
- Guided imagery
- Massage therapy
- Music or art therapy
- Spirituality
- Aerobic exercise

Relying solely on these therapies is generally not enough to treat depression. They may be helpful when used in addition to medication and psychotherapy.

Coping and Support

Talk with your doctor or therapist about improving your coping skills, and try these tips:

- Simplify your life. Cut back on obligations when possible, and set reasonable goals for yourself. Give yourself permission to do less when you feel down.
- Write in a journal. Journaling, as part of your treatment, may improve mood by allowing you to express pain, anger, fear or other emotions.
- Read reputable self-help books and websites. Your doctor or therapist may be able to recommend books or websites to read.
- Locate helpful groups. Many organizations, such as the National Alliance on Mental Illness (NAMI) and the Depression and Bipolar Support Alliance, offer education, support groups, counseling and other resources to help with depression. Employee assistance programs and religious groups also may offer help for mental health concerns.
- Don't become isolated. Try to participate in social activities, and get together with family or friends regularly. Support groups for people with depression can help you connect to others facing similar challenges and share experiences.
- Learn ways to relax and manage your stress. Examples include meditation, progressive muscle relaxation, yoga and tai chi.

- Structure your time. Plan your day. You may find it helps to make a list of daily tasks, use sticky notes as reminders or use a planner to stay organized.
- Don't make important decisions when you're down. Avoid decision-making when you're feeling depressed, since you may not be thinking clearly.

Depression Counseling

Counseling meant for helping people to cope up with depression is known as depression counseling.

There are many benefits of depression counseling. But before determining whether or not you specifically will benefit from depression counseling, it is important to first note that it is common to feel sad, lonely, or depressed at different points in your life. These are typical emotions and common reactions to hard or tough times in life. Therefore, those who receive the greatest benefit from depression counseling usually suffer from symptoms of depression for weeks or months at a time and/or are experiencing symptoms that impact their ability to effectively handle day-to-day tasks and activities.

Counseling aims to assist you to understand why and how depression may be occurring at this time. Feeling depressed can be a very lonely time, and you may think that nobody understands how you are feeling. It can be hard to feel that things will ever get better. The aim of counseling is to provide a supportive and safe environment and to provide therapy and strategies that research has shown to be effective in lifting depression.

Depending on your circumstances, your counseling may include a program to help you increase activity and exercise, assertiveness and relaxation.

References

- Symptoms-causes, diseases-conditions, depression, syc-20356007: mayoclinic.org, Retrieved 11 April 2018
- What-is-depression, patients-families, depression: psychiatry.org, Retrieved 10 March 2018
- Depression-causes-symptoms-treatments-8933: medicalnewstoday.com, Retrieved 30 March 2018
- Depression.central: psycom.net, Retrieved 23 July 2018
- What-is-depression-counseling: onlinecounselling.com, Retrieved 13 May 2018

Career Counseling

Career counseling involved giving advice and guidance regarding career change, career exploration, and career development. Career counselors assists in making good choices of career by putting a person's aptitudes, weaknesses, qualification, hobbies, job prospects, etc. in a broad perspective. This chapter investigates the importance of career counseling in the modern scenario and also discusses about career development and guidance, career counseling process, Holland's Theory, etc.

Career counseling is now a days an emerging field in counseling, which gives relevant information regarding different career. Career counseling is now being increasingly stressed as an integral part of education. In order to secure the right job, the right career choice is foremost in the minds of every job seeker with /with out professional qualifications. The demands of the modern age are very complex.

The original approach to formal vocational counseling is generally traced back to Frank Parsons (1909). Parsons became interested in unemployed school leavers and developed a counseling service in the Boston Civic House, a social settlement. In 1909, he published a book (Choosing a Vocation) in which he structured the three steps of vocational counseling as he viewed them in practice: self-analysis, occupational analysis, and true reasoning or counseling to relate personal and occupational information. Since Parsons' original contribution, a variety of approaches to career counseling have been developed representing a rich range of intellectual perspectives. Differential, developmental, social learning, cognitive, sociological, economic, and mathematical models have all been used.

Career Counseling can be defined as the process of helping and enabling people in their career development. Career counseling and guidance may involve both face-to-face help or may be mediated through telephone, letter, text, or through internet. However, most important of all remains the one-to-one interview between the career counselor and the client. A career counselor would be facing clients who are making career decisions and choices or coping with life changes, which relate to their working life -- career changes, redundancy and unemployment.

In 1981, Crites used this model and methods of career counseling to define the unique parameters of a given career counseling approach and provide a schema for synthesizing the approaches (trait-and-factor, client-centered, psychodynamic, developmental, and behavioral). The methods of career counseling are more pragmatic than theoretical and attempt to translate the model into operational terms. They include the interview techniques used by the counselor, the test-interpretation procedures engaged in by the client and counselor, and the acquisition and use of occupational information.

Career Counseling is a life long process since the individual choose an occupation, prepare for it, and make progress in it. Career Counseling has to do with knowing their interest, selection of their subject, formation of their study habit and make them progress in those subject and activities and attain the ultimate aim of getting good career as per their wish.

It is concerned primarily with helping the individual to make decisions and choices involved in planning for future and to form career decisions and choice necessary in affecting career adjustment. It stands to take necessary care of the interest of the individual.

Career counseling is a personalized process that combines both intuitive and cognitive techniques to help to understand oneself, explore career options, and clarify and attain desired career goals. The processes of career counseling offer insight, guidance and support to help students to understand and manage different career and lifestyle issues.

The following five assumptions underlie the trait-factor conception of vocational development:

- Vocational development is largely a cognitive process in which the individual uses reasoning to arrive at his decision.
- Occupational choice is a single event.
- There is a single right goal for everyone making decisions about work.
- A single type of person works in each job.
- There is an occupational choice available to each individual.

Career counseling and guidance generally involves face-to-face interaction and interaction through telephone, letters, or Internet. However, most important of all is the one-to-one interaction between the career counselor and the client. A career counselor deals with people who are making career decisions and choices or coping with changes like- choice of subjects, career changes, and redundancy. The matter of career decision, and a student's direction and progress towards professional goals often play a crucial role in the development of individual identity and purpose, as well as positive self-esteem and inter-personal functioning.

Career counseling acts as a process of self-exploration and interest, identification of the client and helps in career choice and decision-making. Career counseling, thus spans both the internal psychology of the person and external context of education and employment.

Career counselor helps the students to evaluate their abilities, interests, talents and personality characteristic to develop realistic academic and career goals. Career counselor also helps the individuals make career decisions after exploring and evaluating their education, training, work experience, interest, skills and personal traits and arrange for aptitude and achievement tests. This helps the individual to develop job search skills such as resume writing and interviewing techniques.

Career counselors should know in broad terms how one occupational field differs from another and the different levels each jobs within each field. A wide knowledge of career opportunities is essential for career counselors, so that the counselor will be able to give appropriate suggestions at the career planning stage and also assesses the client's view of the opportunities and can be provide information on existing career. Based on the client's wish, counselor can help him/her to choose a career according to his/her wish.

Holland's Theory

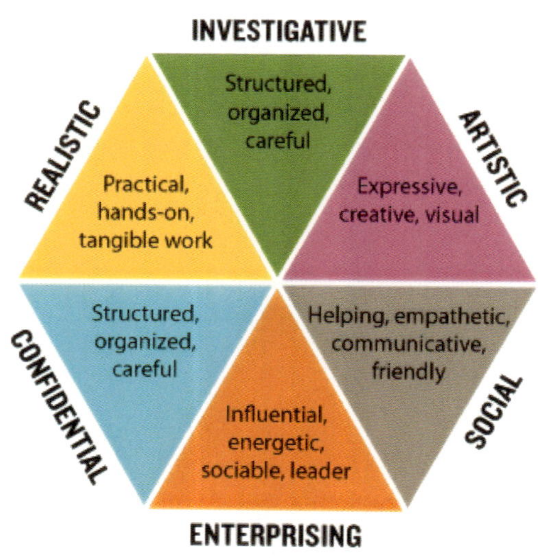

Careers are determined by an interaction between our personality and the environment in John Holland's Theory of Career Choice. We want jobs with people like us.

John Holland's Theory of Career Choice (RIASEC) maintains that in choosing a career, people prefer jobs where they can be around others who are like them. They search for environments that will let them use their skills and abilities, and express their attitudes and values, while taking on enjoyable problems and roles. Behaviors are determined by an interaction between personality and environment.

Holland's theory is centered on the notion that most people fit into one of six personality types:

- Realistic
- Investigative
- Artistic
- Social
- Enterprising
- Conventional.

Realistic

- Description of interest area:

Likes to work mainly with hands, making, fixing, assembling or building things, using and operating equipment, tools or machines. Often likes to work outdoors.

- Some key skills:

Using and operating tools, equipment and machinery, designing, building, repairing, maintaining, working manually, measuring, working in detail, driving, moving, caring for animals, working with plants.

- Some occupations with Realistic components:

Pilot, farmer, horticulturalist, builder, engineer, armed services personnel, mechanic, upholsterer, electrician, computer technologist, park ranger, sportsperson.

- Subjects one could study to get related skills:

English, Maths, Science, Workshop, Technology, Computing, Business Studies, Agriculture, Horticulture, Physical Education.

Investigative

- Description of interest area:

Likes to discover and research ideas, observe, investigate and experiment, ask questions and solve problems.

- Some key skills:

Thinking analytically and logically, computing, communicating by writing and speaking, designing, formulating, calculating, diagnosing, experimenting, investigating.

- Some occupations with Investigative components:

Science, research, medical and health occupations, chemist, marine scientist, forestry technician, medical or agricultural laboratory technician, zoologist, dentist, doctor.

- Subjects one could study to get related skills:

English, Maths, Science, Computing, Technology.

Artistic

- Description of interest area:

Likes to use words, art, music or drama to communicate, perform, or express themselves, create and design things.

- Some key skills:

Expressing artistically or physically, speaking, writing, singing, performing, designing, presenting, planning, composing, playing, dancing.

- Some occupations with Artistic components:

Artist, illustrator, photographer, sign writer, composer, singer, instrument player, dancer, actor, reporter, writer, editor, advertiser, hairdresser, fashion designer.

- Subjects one could study to get related skills:

English, Social Studies, Music, Drama, Art, Graphic Design, Computing, Business Studies, Languages.

Social

- Description of interest area:

Likes to work with people to teach, train and inform, help, treat, heal and cure, serve and greet, concerned for the wellbeing and welfare of others.

- Some key skills:

Communicating orally or in writing, caring and supporting, training, meeting, greeting, assisting, teaching, informing, interviewing, coaching.

- Some occupations with Social components:

Teacher, nurse, nurse aide, counselor, police officer, social worker, salesperson, customer service officer, waiter, secretary.

- Subjects one could study to get related skills:

English, Social Studies, Maths, Science, Health, Physical Education, Art, Computing, Business Studies, Languages.

Enterprising

- Description of interest area:

Likes meeting people, leading, talking to and influencing others, encouraging others, working in business.

- Some key skills:

Selling, promoting and persuading, developing ideas, public speaking, managing, organizing, leading and captaining, computing, planning.

- Some occupations with Enterprising components:

Salesperson, lawyer, politician, accountant, business owner, executive or manager, travel agent, music or sports promoter.

- Subjects one could study to get related skills:

English, Maths, Business Studies, Accounting, Economics, Social Studies, Drama, Computing, Text Information Management, Languages.

Conventional

- Description of interest area:

Likes working indoors and at tasks that involve organizing and being accurate, following procedures, working with data or numbers, planning work and events.

- Some key skills:

Computing and keyboarding, recording and keeping records, paying attention to detail, meeting and greeting, doing calculations, handling money, organizing, arranging, working independently.

- Some occupations with Conventional components:

Secretary, receptionist, office worker, librarian, bank clerk, computer operator, stores and dispatch clerk.

- Subjects one could study to get related skills:

English, Maths, Business Studies, Accounting, Economics, Computing, Text Information Management.

Holland asserts that people of the same personality type working together in a job create an environment that fits and rewards their type.

Within this theory there are six basic types of work environment, which correlate directly to the personality types. Holland emphasizes that people who choose to work in an environment similar to their personality type are more likely to be successful and satisfied. This idea is important as it shows Holland's theory can be flexible, incorporating combination types.

Holland's theory takes a problem-solving and cognitive approach to career planning. His model has been very influential in career counseling. It has been employed through popular assessment tools such as the Self-Directed Search, Vocational Preference Inventory and the Strong Interest Inventory.

Process of Career Counseling

Getting to Know you

The first stage of your counseling is known as the initiation stage. Here you will get to know your counselor and he will get to know you. At this stage it is vital to start building up a rapport with your chosen mentor or coach. If the relationship is not going to work, then you need to seek an alternative counselor. This will be through no fault of your own. But, having a counselor you are comfortable talking too is extremely important.

Gathering of Data

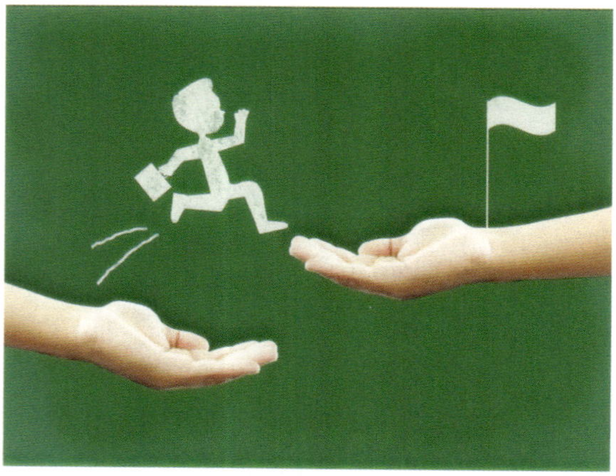

This stage will involve both yourself and your caregivers or parents. Data needs to be gathered so that a picture of who you are can be built up. This is done in various ways including questionnaires and form filling. This part of the process may seem a little boring, but it is essential that your counselor understands not just who you are now, but where you have come from to reach where you are.

Awareness

This is an extremely important stage of career counseling. By this stage, you will be comfortable with your chosen coach or mentor, and your counselor will know a lot about you. With this knowledge, he is then able to start working towards steps and strategies that he will use throughout the remaining stages of your counseling. At this stage, your rapport with your counselor should be excellent, and you should feel relaxed and comfortable with your sessions. If you do not, then you have not chosen a good career counselor. If you are having doubts at this stage, then your chosen counselor may be lacking in expertise.

Exploration

With stage one now complete, you will move swiftly onto the exploration stage. By now you will know for sure you have chosen the best counselor. During this stage, you will conduct an analysis, with the help of your mentor. This analytical stage will include some tests, and you will have your social behavior assessed, as well as your personality and your career interests. With this information, and your job experience discussed, it is time to move on to a one on one interaction with your counselor that will allow you to discover what avenues and paths are open to you.

Decision Making

By this stage, different paths will have been explored, and a decision needs to be made. You, your counselor, and your parents will need to reach a common ground. Any barriers that are stopping you for choosing a career will be ruled out. The most appropriate options will be selected for your career, and a critical decision will be made. It is at this stage where parents and children would, without counseling, come to heads. Parents often expect their children to follow in their footsteps, accepting any other choice as a failure. Correct counseling will explore which path is actually the right one for you, and not just for your parents.

Preparation

At this stage, all avenues will have been explored and decisions will have been made. Now is the time to prepare a plan of action. This plan will allow you to go down your chose route and succeed. Resources necessary will be made available at this stage, as well as a backup plan. All the best counselors have a backup plan.

Final Stage

The final stage is the implementation of the plan. You will be given goals, and deadlines to achieve. This is perhaps for you the most exciting stage and perhaps for your counselor the most nerve-racking too! Both he and you will be hoping that all the hard work you have put in will get you to the place you want to be in your life, and that you will no longer be stuck at a crossroads.

Career Counseling in Schools

Career counseling in schools ensures the right kind of help to overcome such thinking and stop students from making such mistakes. Many students take a psychometric test in order to avoid making mistakes and their efforts are commendable, although the results of the test might leave them more confused than before. Why? The psychometric test basically outlines the strengths and weaknesses of students and highlights their aptitudes and interests. The catch is, their aptitudes and interests don't necessary have to match. Meaning, they can be good at Math but have an interest in Arts. So which career option do they pick?

An established career counselor will firstly, be able to explain the entire report, tell them the perks and disadvantages of pursuing both their interests and aptitudes, and give them the clarity and understanding to make the right decisions. This is much needed, especially, when students are prone to taking advice from inexperienced sources.

Students tend to take advice from anyone they think has an experience. But it may not always be right or let alone be the best one. The path followed by their seemingly successful peers might not help them to reach the same destination, their model adults must have gone through failures themselves and their parents might be unaware of the latest industry demands. To make sure that students have clarity of thought, career counselors must be made available for students at all times while they are in high school to receive the right and latest advice.

Some countries have made it compulsory for schools to have counselors, there still needs to be a distinction made as to what kind of counselors are required. Many of the counselors already present are life skill counselors and although life skills are important, the number of college advisors (counselors) is low. Ultimately, college advisors are what students need most to be successful. To highlight, the urgent requirement for career counselors recent stats show a whopping 92% of students who don't get any career-related guidance from their schools.

Decisions made in High School often make or break a student's career. Experienced career counselors are trained to understand students thinking and their potential. Once a student's potential is understood, the counselor is able to guide the student to the best career suitable to him/her and help them make the decisions that ensure career success.

Students want to be successful and they don't mind getting help. They may feel shy at first or think it's weak to take help, but it is our responsibility to help them build strong careers. Having a career counseling cell in schools is the first step in doing that. It is a great first step indeed.

Importance of Career Counseling

Career Counseling helps in determining a student's true potential. Students are often confused about their career preferences. Aptitude tests and counseling sessions would help identify their field of specialization. This would indeed help a student in following the right course of study for accomplishing his career goal.

Secondly, despite having a clear idea of their choice of career, students do not have the requisite knowledge to plan their higher course of specialized study in order to fulfill the eligibility for their chosen field. In such a scenario, career counseling can help clear these doubts by giving them clarity and vision regarding what they can expect from various educational courses. Sometimes, students have pre-conceived ideas about certain fields. Counseling would help build in awareness by putting things in the right perspective.

Students are often overwhelmed by the prospect of change and the chain of events that lead to their eventual admission for higher studies. At such times, the essential support provided by the counselor throughout the admission process can boost their morale and give them the confidence to face all odds. Counselors play a crucial role in building the motivational level of students, which is necessary for long-term success. Career counseling also teaches students ways and means to expand their network, which in turn enhances emotional support during their course of higher study.

While college truly is about overall development of a student's personality, counseling at an early stage could help one gain the right perspective, especially with the number of new career options coming up every day, which would otherwise not be considered by students. Early counseling assists students in reflecting on their personalities and abilities, likes and dislikes, and how these would align with various career paths. This would help students have a focused approach in their search for a suitable University for continuing their higher education and realizing their career aspirations.

Under the guidance of an experienced counselor, students attain calm confidence and focused ambition for achieving success in their chosen field.

Career Counselor

Career Counselors are professionals who hold degrees in related areas, such as Counseling or Psychology, who have chosen to concentrate in the field of career development. Their strength is the academic training they receive in counseling, helping them to understand how different personalities work in a professional setting. As counselors advance in education and experience level, there are higher levels of recognition they may receive.

As per the National Career Development Association, a person could be certified on one of the following levels as a Career Counselor.

1. The National Certified Career Counselor is a title held by a person who has a graduate degree in counseling or a related professional field from an accredited institution, completed supervised counseling experience which included career counseling, acquired a minimum of three years of full-time career development work experience, and successfully completed a knowledge-based certification examination.

2. In 1999, the NCDA retired this title, and made all who held it into Master Career Counselors. Other qualifications, professionals hold a master's degree in counseling or related field and have been active as an NCDA member for a minimum of two years. An MCC has at least three years of experience in career counseling and must successfully complete a supervised career counseling practicum. MCCs are skilled in administering and interpreting career assessments and provide the highest quality of career counseling services.

3. The Master Career Development Professional (MCDP) is an NCDA member who holds a master's degree or higher in counseling or related field. The MCDP has at least three years of postmaster's career development experience in training, teaching, program development, or materials development.

4. The Fellow is an NCDA member of professional distinction. A Fellow designation recognizes outstanding and substantial contributions to career development in science, teaching and training, practice, service, policy development, and political action.

Searching for a professional to help improve any aspect of your life takes time. It is important to know about the person's qualifications, experience, and style of practice. Even though all counselors are different, and your session should be tailored to your specific needs, there are some actions that all counselors should be able to perform:

- Conduct personal counseling sessions to help you clarify career goals
- Administer and interpret tests to assess your skills and interests, to help identify career options

- Plan career exploratory activities through assignments
- Provide exercises for improving decision-making skills
- Help you to develop a personal career plan
- Teach strategies for job search- Skills and assist in the development of resumes
- Provide support for those experiencing job stress, job loss, and career transition

Career Development and Guidances

Career development is the process that forms a person's work identity. It is a significant part of human development and spans over the individual's entire lifetime, beginning when the individual first becomes aware of how people make a living. For example, when a child notices that some people are doctors, others are firefighters, and some are carpenters, it signals the start of this process. It continues as that person begins to explore occupations and ultimately decides what career to pursue him- or herself.

Career development doesn't end there. After you choose a profession, you must then get the required education and training, apply for and find employment, and ultimately advance in your career. For most people, it will also include changing careers and jobs at least once during their work lives, but probably more often than that.

It is important to note that, for most individuals, career development occurs without any intervention from other people. There also isn't a set age for when it will begin—some people will start to think about occupational choices very early in life, while others won't give this subject much thought until they are relatively close to having to decide how they will earn money.

While many individuals go through this process independently, almost everyone can benefit greatly from getting expert career guidance. Advice from a career counselor or other similarly trained specialist, or taking a class in school that helps with career development, allows you forge a more satisfying and successful career path. This type of intervention can begin as early as elementary school, and it should continue throughout adulthood. Many people find themselves in need of professional advice as they encounter problems or must make decisions about their careers, for instance when they are thinking of looking for a new job or changing occupations.

Factors and Barriers that Influence Career Development

Several factors and the interactions between them influence career development. Others may be barriers to it. Let's look at several of them:

- Personal Characteristics: Personality type, interests, aptitudes, and work-related values make all of us who we are. These personal characteristics play a significant role in career development since they influence which occupations we find satisfying, as well as the types of work environments in which we will succeed. That is why, when you are in the process of choosing a career, it is so important to do a self-assessment that will help you learn all about yourself.
- Financial Resources: Pursuing certain career options can be costly. If you choose an occupation, for example, that requires you to attend college; you may be limited by your ability to pay for it. You could end up altering your plans. Fortunately, there are ways of overcoming barriers such as limited financial resources, namely student loans, financial aid, and scholarships. When you are seeking employment, financial limitations can also hinder you. For example, you may not have the money to purchase interview attire. Several organizations collect donations of professional clothing and distribute it to job seekers in need.
- Financial Obligations: You may find yourself working in a job or occupation just for the paycheck. It lets you keep up with your bills but doesn't satisfy you in any other way. You would like to go after other opportunities but feel inhibited by your financial obligations such as a mortgage, rent, student loans, or even your children's college tuition. You can try to put away money for a future career change or even change your way of life by downsizing to a smaller home.
- Physical, Mental, and Emotional Impairments: Some of us are better suited to some careers than we are to others due to our physical and mental abilities, and limitations. For example, you may want to become a doctor but don't have the intellectual ability to get into medical school. You should, if possible, find a related occupation that makes the best use your strengths while accommodating your limitations.

- Lack of Support From Family: Going after a hard-to-achieve goal is even more difficult if your loved ones aren't behind you. You have a greater chance of succeeding if you can convince them to become your cheerleaders but if that is unlikely to happen, you may have to find motivation from other people in your life.
- Age: Our age, or our perception of it, can hinder us in our career development. During a large part of our lives, we may worry about being too young to pursue a particular path, advance in our careers, or make a career change, and for another lengthy stretch, we fret about being too old to do those things. Instead of focusing on your age, concentrate on your abilities and how motivated you are.
- Family Obligations: An individual's career development may stall if he or she takes time off from work to take care of children or elderly parents. He or she has several options including getting outside help to provide childcare or eldercare if the individual desires it.

Career guidance consists of services that help people successfully manage their career development. Career development, an aspect of human development, is the process through which an individual's work identity emerges. Although it will occur on its own as you mature, you may benefit from getting assistance as you navigate through this process, which can be quite confusing at times.

Many people seek out assistance from career development professionals only when they are trying to choose a career for the first time, or perhaps when they are going through a transition. The intent of career guidance, however, is to provide support to individuals throughout their entire lives. Let's take a look at when, during your career, you should get help.

Far too many people are dissatisfied with what they do for a living. They make mistakes when choosing a career and end up in an occupation that isn't a good fit. That's not surprising since going through the career planning process, including the four steps one should take when choosing a career, is difficult. It may seem like it would just be easier to pick an occupation out of a hat.

While making a random choice may be simpler, it is certainly not wise. Given the amount of time you spend at work, you should do everything possible to make a well-informed decision. Getting help from a professional who provides career guidance can be the difference between ending up in a satisfying career or one that makes you miserable.

A career development professional, such as a career counselor, may use self-assessment instruments to help you learn about your interests, values, skills, and personality type. After coming up with a list of occupations that seem suitable for you based on the results, he or she can show you how to explore them and then weed out the ones that are not as good a fit as others. Then, the counselor can help you create a career action plan that will allow you to pursue the occupation you chose.

What is the point of choosing a vocation if you don't know how to find a job? Career guidance also consists of providing job search assistance when you are looking for your first job or any subsequent ones. The way in which we look for work has changed significantly over the last decades, and it continues to change. Career guidance professionals keep up-to-date on the best methods to use when job searching.

A career counselor will show you what resources to use to locate job announcements. He or she will help you write an effective resume and will teach you how to network. When it comes time to go on job interviews, you can also get advice on how to best answer questions and negotiate a job offer.

Get Mid-Career Advice

In addition to getting help with matters that involve beginning your career, such as choosing a vocation or securing your first job, you can also get direction about things that occur later. For example, career guidance services also include helping individuals advance their careers and deal with workplace issues.

A career development professional can answer your questions about career advancement. He or she can tell you what to do to be promoted or get a raise, or even help you decide whether to quit your job. You can get advice about getting along with co-workers and your boss, preparing for and responding to performance reviews, and managing job stress and burnout.

Get Help If you Lose your Job

Job loss is devastating both financially and emotionally. When you lose your job, a piece of your identity is also taken away. The most tangible result, however, is the loss of income. Assisting those who are dealing with this devastating life change is a component of career guidance. Since you probably don't want to spend extra money when you are already feeling distressed about your finances, you should look into free or low-cost career guidance services.

A career counselor or other advisor can assist newly unemployed clients to cope with practical issues like applying for unemployment benefits and continuing health insurance. Eventually, he or she can help the client begin the job search process. They can also get encouragement and advice from professionals and, through support groups, from others who are in the same situation.

Get Advice About Making a Career Change

Since most people do not stay in the same occupation for their entire working lives—some individuals even switch careers multiple times—there will probably come a time when you will want to make a change. A career guidance professional can give you advice when you are taking on this kind of transition.

Meet with a career development specialist who can help you assess your transferable skills. With their assistance, you can discover what skills you can bring to your new occupation and which ones you will need to acquire before you can begin a new career.

Get Motivation

When you are engaged in the day-to-day activities of making a living, searching for a new job, or making another change, sometimes you just need an unbiased cheerleader by your side. Your partner, friends, and family have a stake in your future and may have difficulty being impartial. For example, if you need encouragement to make a big career change but your partner is worried about how it will affect your finances, a professional advisor who doesn't have any skin in the game can be just what you need.

Career guidance professional can motivate you when things aren't going the way you would like. He or she will encourage you not to give up whether you are stuck in an unsuccessful job search campaign or having trouble making a decision about leaving a career behind and pursuing a new one, even if it will be difficult to retrain. They can give you a realistic look at what to expect, tell you whether you are making a wise decision, and cheer you on when you feel like giving up.

Where Can You Get Career Guidance

Professionals who provide career guidance include career counselors and career development facilitators. School guidance counselors provide these services to middle and high school students, who can get an early start on making career-related decisions. A college student can seek career counseling from the career services office at his or her institution.

Career centers in public libraries are a good source of free career planning assistance. Librarians can teach you to use all the resources and tools. Many also have counseling services available. In addition, many community agencies provide free or low-cost vocational assistance, including occupational training programs and workshops on job search skills.

References

- Hollands-theory, career-theory-models, career-practice: careers.govt.nz, Retrieved 11 July 2018
- Process-of-career-counselling: chriskenber.com, Retrieved 28 March 2018
- Importance-of-career-counselling-collegepond: collegepond.com, Retrieved 19 April 2018
- What-is-career-development-525496: thebalancecareers.com, Retrieved 10 May 2018
- What-is-career-guidance-525498: thebalancecareers.com, Retrieved 25 June 2018

Permissions

All chapters in this book are published with permission under the Creative Commons Attribution Share Alike License or equivalent. Every chapter published in this book has been scrutinized by our experts. Their significance has been extensively debated. The topics covered herein carry significant information for a comprehensive understanding. They may even be implemented as practical applications or may be referred to as a beginning point for further studies.

We would like to thank the editorial team for lending their expertise to make the book truly unique. They have played a crucial role in the development of this book. Without their invaluable contributions this book wouldn't have been possible. They have made vital efforts to compile up to date information on the varied aspects of this subject to make this book a valuable addition to the collection of many professionals and students.

This book was conceptualized with the vision of imparting up-to-date and integrated information in this field. To ensure the same, a matchless editorial board was set up. Every individual on the board went through rigorous rounds of assessment to prove their worth. After which they invested a large part of their time researching and compiling the most relevant data for our readers.

The editorial board has been involved in producing this book since its inception. They have spent rigorous hours researching and exploring the diverse topics which have resulted in the successful publishing of this book. They have passed on their knowledge of decades through this book. To expedite this challenging task, the publisher supported the team at every step. A small team of assistant editors was also appointed to further simplify the editing procedure and attain best results for the readers.

Apart from the editorial board, the designing team has also invested a significant amount of their time in understanding the subject and creating the most relevant covers. They scrutinized every image to scout for the most suitable representation of the subject and create an appropriate cover for the book.

The publishing team has been an ardent support to the editorial, designing and production team. Their endless efforts to recruit the best for this project, has resulted in the accomplishment of this book. They are a veteran in the field of academics and their pool of knowledge is as vast as their experience in printing. Their expertise and guidance has proved useful at every step. Their uncompromising quality standards have made this book an exceptional effort. Their encouragement from time to time has been an inspiration for everyone.

The publisher and the editorial board hope that this book will prove to be a valuable piece of knowledge for students, practitioners and scholars across the globe.

Index